The Digital Evolution of Live Music

The Digital Evolution of Live Music

Editors

Angela Cresswell Jones and Rebecca Jane Bennett

ELSEVIER

AMSTERDAM • BOSTON • CAMBRIDGE • HEIDELBERG
LONDON • NEW YORK • OXFORD • PARIS • SAN DIEGO
SAN FRANCISCO • SINGAPORE • SYDNEY • TOKYO
Chandos Publishing is an imprint of Elsevier

CP
CHANDOS PUBLISHING

Acquiring Editor: George Knott
Editorial Project Manager: Harriet Clayton
Project Manager: Preethy J Mampally
Designer: Mark Rogers

Chandos Publishing is an imprint of Elsevier
225 Wyman Street, Waltham, MA 02451, USA
Langford Lane, Kidlington, OX5 1GB, UK

British Library Cataloguing in Publication Data
A catalogue record for this book is available from the British Library

Library of Congress Cataloging-in-Publication Data
A catalog record for this book is available from the Library of Congress

ISBN 978-0-08-100067-0

For information on all Chandos Publishing visit our website at http://store.elsevier.com/

Printed and bound in the United Kingdom

Contents

Preface

The concept of "live" has morphed and changed in mediated culture. From the invention of the telegraph, "live" has been transformed by our increasingly sophisticated ability to interact in "real time," without necessarily sharing physical corporeal space with others. In a *digitally* mediated culture, where convergent hand held and pocket technologies mean that multi-media access is ubiquitous, "live" is becoming increasingly connected to notions of "real time," especially as people are also becoming increasingly comfortable interacting in virtual space. Nowadays, a "virtual-live experience" can be captured or undergone, quite literally, at our fingertips.

A quick Google search for definitions of "live" embodies (pun intended) an intimate, co-dependent, and reciprocal relationship between "performance" and technology. The paradox evident in the definition offered by popular web dictionary, *dictionary.com*, has repercussions that extend into contemporary experiences of musical texts, economy and theory. *Dictionary.com* defines "live," as it pertains to performance, as "being at an actual event or performance: the match will be televised live."[1] From this contemporary, digitized popular understanding of the term, it appears that the experience of live music could soon do away with flesh altogether. Internet semantics, as well as the marketing and production of virtual "live-music" and suggestions that "live" can be televised, indicates that time may eventually overwhelm the connection between "live" and the physical body. Or will it?

This manuscript considers notions of live music in digitally influenced time and space and posits that, unlike the "on off" binary function, experiences of "live music" in digital culture dance on the borders between mind and body, words and feelings, sight and sound, virtual and real, individual and communal, and online and offline. It argues that the face-to-face corporeal live musical experience has not been usurped or replaced, but that it occupies an important and multi-modal role in a cultural contextual landscape whose shape is forever changing, thanks to the evolution of technological invention.

Angela Jones
Rebecca Bennett

[1] Dictionary.com. *Live*. http://dictionary.reference.com/browse/live (Accessed 1/6/2012)

Introduction

From the family tree of old school hip hop
Kick off your shoes and relax your socks
The rhymes will spread just like a pox
Cause the music is live like an electric shock

The Beastie Boys (1998).

All media work us over completely. They are so pervasive in there personal, political, economic, aesthetic, psychological, moral, ethical and social consequences that they leave no part of us untouched, unaffected, unaltered. The medium is the massage. Any understanding of social and cultural change is impossible without knowledge of the way media work as environments. All media are extensions of some human faculty-psychic or physical.

McLuhan et al. (1967), p. 26.

Given the rapid pace of technological change, especially in the digital era, any book investigating digital culture is a history text by the time it reaches the shelves. As Conner remarks, "technology forecasts tend to become outdated, if not entirely quaint, within hours of publication" (Conner, 2013, p. 17); yet, outdated or not, it is important to regularly press pause and take the time to reflect upon moments that would otherwise be swallowed up in the rush to the future. Fuelled by a desire to take stock of and memorialize social and cultural activities that infuse our everyday lives with meaning, this book seeks to re-examine the role of live music through the lens of a rapidly evolving digital culture.

Music and digital technology have much in common, in that both forms have the power to alter our experience of linear time and material space. Like following a link to a completely different website, a particular song can transport us back in time to the moment it first held meaning, or it can trigger an emotion or "feeling" that is less easy to place. Like the nonlinear, hypertext experience familiar to digital experience, this book offers a mash-up of various perspectives of the articulation between digital technology and live music.

The digital evolution

The speed at which digital technology allows people to communicate, and the increasingly sophisticated mediums through which this communication takes place, means that much of life can, and is, being lived through the screen. This *new* participatory culture enabled through the interactive features of digital technology has been the focus of a diverse body of scholarly work, dedicated to tracking the evolution and cultural ramifications of this "new media." This book contributes to this expanding conversation by examining how musical consumption and enjoyment in an increasingly elastic conception of the "live" form functions "in an era of musical 'abundance,' in which both historical and contemporary recordings are increasingly accessible" (Sexton, 2009, p. 99).

Live music

Music is a powerful social tool, beyond that of cultural and subcultural affiliations and identity making, or recreational practices. "It arouses emotions, evokes memories and builds bonds—music touches people" (Unterstell, 2012, p. 20). While an abundance of enjoyment can be gained through listening to recorded music, live music changes and extends the rules of engagement by transforming the experience of music from that of a listener into that of an audience member. Thus "live-music" augments repeatable individualized and deeply personal auditory experience of the solitary listener, and re-frames it and re-energizes it by transforming it into the communal experience with the capacity to engage all of the senses at once.

The live music economy

Live music is not just about the multi-sensual communal experience, it is also a form of cultural engagement that has a history reaching as far back as the records of human art and culture. It is only in the recent past, since the advent of digital technology and the decline of the "old" media economy, that it has become a central feature of the "new" musical economy (Holt, 2010, pp. 242–261). Lee reported that in the decade between 1999 and 2009, the sale of tickets to live music events in the United States rose from $1.5 billion to $6.4 billion, which was "vastly exceeding the growth of inflation and population growth" (2012). He also noted that as global wealth grows and further economic constraints are placed on the movement of resources, "a growing share of our disposable incomes are going to be devoted to experiences rather than manufactured products" (Lee, 2012). With diminished returns for individual music releases, live music has replaced the sale of music as the driving force in this new cultural economy, and whilst established artists may have experienced diminished sales as a result of digital music distribution, this has been offset by the increased viability and profitability of touring.

The increasing financial viability and likelihood of success for touring has been a defining characteristic of what has been labeled the "live music renaissance" (Apostolou, 2012). In an age of information surplus, niche markets are becoming increasingly viable and accessible, and artists and promoters operating in these markets have recognized that touring and live performance hold significant financial benefits that outweigh any likely profit from music sales. The proliferation of an increasingly live-music saturated cultural landscape has had significant ramifications for the ways in which we consume music, and the cultures that exist, and have developed, around the live music form.

Live music and digital culture

The so-called live music renaissance is supported by, rather than counter to, the growing familiarity with and use of digital technology in everyday life. The live music economy extends far beyond the revenue generated from ticket sales. Rather, digital technology plays a key role in the celebration of the live music form, with a myriad of interactive and social cyber-spaces dedicated to the celebration and promotion of live music events. From the local gig to the global festival, live music is streamed, shared, uploaded, downloaded, reviewed, watched, and re-watched online. Therefore, any analysis of live music must take into account the increasing power that Web 2.0 and 3.0 technologies lend to the form.

In a time where fans have the capacity to communicate with one another and access live-streamed concerts or footage from wherever they happen to be in material space through mobile smartphones and tablets, we argue that it is no longer viable to conceive of online and offline as representing mutually exclusive categories. As Auslander (1999) attests, all live performances are forced by economic reality to acknowledge their status as media within a mediatic system that includes mass media and information technologies (p. 4). Thus, it follows that today's mobile Internet technologies alter the conventions of live performance itself.

Today, there are multiple ways that audiences can use digital technology to participate in "live performance," from the posting of pictures and video footage on social media, to the emergence of tweet seats, or using a smartphone application meeting to plan itineraries at music festivals. Thanks to digital technologies, the definition of "live music" has also expanded to include a number of forms that do not require the artist and audience to share the same space or even the same time. Sanden's recent definition embraces the complexity of the notion of liveness today. He suggests that

> *In any given musical performance context, liveness can emerge in a variety of ways. We may experience liveness as a condition of temporality or spatial proximity. We may consider musical sound to be live in its fidelity to an original or ideal "true" utterance. We may interpret liveness as a quality of spontaneity, thought to reside especially in the uniqueness of individual performances. We may encounter liveness as a trace of corporeality, as an indication of musical interactivity, or as a condition of some other perceptual category ….*
>
> *Sanden (2013), p. 159.*

It is with this broad scope for interpretation that the authors who comprise this book approached their chapters. And the multiple ways that liveness can be interpreted in a digital culture, means that each chapter tells a unique story, which offers insight into the diverse experiences our culture of musical and digital abundance affords. Taking us on this journey is a diverse range of authors, exploring a wide range of topics, which together compose a pastiche of interpretations of the single theme that holds the book together: *the increasingly interdependent relationship between live music and digital culture.*

The title of this book, *The Digital Evolution of Live Music*, does not refer to an evolution in a linear sense, but a philosophical one. With a broad focus on contemporary manifestations of the relationship between live music and digital culture, the authors explore the reciprocal relationship between digital and musical texts evoking discussions of "live" which transcend economic boundaries to challenge and/or reinforce analog expressions of corporeality, genre, time, and fandom. This book is split into three sections: "Live that survives," "Digital live," and "Live after death." The overarching narrative considers: how digital technology influences the function of live music in its traditional sense, as a one-off concert event in material space and real time; how new definitions and experiences of live music are emerging from digital culture, which alter the definition of "liveness" itself; and finally, how digital technology has created live musical experiences that connect audiences and listeners to death, by resurrecting "dead" music and "dead" musicians.

Through the exploration of fandom, identity, and the live music experience, *Live that survives* explores elements of physical live music experiences—sweat, laughs, tears, beers, and voices—that continue to thrive in the transition into an increasingly digital world. The chapters within this section seek to explain and unpack why fans still search and pay for face-to-face unmediated musical experiences. Through discussions of live concerts, from small gigs to large music festivals, these texts look at the significance of the live music culture in terms of fan identity, scene affiliations, and the tangible flesh-to-flesh, immersive experiences that are gained from participation in offline concert culture. Through discussions of jouissance, aura, authenticity, identity, as well as the boundaries of time and space, this section peels back layers of meaning gained from immersion and participation in traditional live concert events and searches for reasons why the live concert experience not only survives, but thrives, in an increasingly digital musical culture.

Digital live focuses on how "live music" is created, experienced, and delivered through digital technology. These chapters present the reader with the musical, theoretical, and personal perspectives of digitally mediated and created liveness, through the eyes and ears of sound theorists, music theorists, musicians, and producers. Through discussions of virtual nightclubs to digital archiving, these chapters focus sharply on participatory culture and explore how live performances manifest, exist, and are shared in digital spaces. Whether it be a musician performing or recording, or the soundtrack of a game moving from the console to the concert hall, these chapters consider what live music means in a context where the boundaries between online and offline; digital and analog, are increasingly hard to find.

Finally, *Live after death* explores the possibilities afforded by digital technology to revive long forgotten musical experiences and artists and to preserve a virtual musical legacy for individuals long after death in the "real" world. The final two pieces in this book take stock of ways in which digital technology acts to resurrect dead music and musicians, as well as its capacity to create a new kind of live artist. In an exploration of folk music, history, collection, appreciation, and archiving, the book's penultimate chapter considers the revival of dead music, afforded through digital technology. It looks at how contemporary artists are making the sounds of once "dead" folk music that is connected to a particular place and time in history live again in the present, in original compositions. The theme of resurrection continues into the final chapter, which looks at the future of the hologram on the live concert stage. By comparing the holographic performance of reincarnated artist, Tupac Shakur, at Coachella in 2012 with the live performances of the anime hologram, Hatsune Miku, this chapter explores the ontological and ethical dimensions of the use of holograms on the live music stage and considers how ready audiences are to accept the technologically generated "artist" as a legitimate and authentic live music performer.

References

Apostolou, N. (2012). *The live music renaissance*. The music network. Retrieved from http://www.themusicnetwork.com/musicfeatures/industry/2012/09/13/thlive-music-renaissance.

Auslander, P. (1999). *Liveness: performance in mediatized culture*. London: Routledge.

Conner, T. (2013). *Masters dissertation: Rei Toei lives!: Hatsune miku and the design of the virtual pop star*. Chicago, Illinois: University of Illinois at Chicago.

Holt, F. (2010). The economy of live music in the digital age. *European Journal of Cultural Studies*, 13, 243–261.

Lee, T. (2012). *Why we shouldn't worry about the (alleged) decline of the music industry*. Forbes. Retrieved from http://www.forbes.com/sites/timothylee/2012/01/30/why-we-shouldnt-worry-about-the-decline-of-the-music-industry.

McLuhan, M., Fiore, Q., & Agel, J. (1967). *The medium is the massage: an inventory of effects*. Ringwood: Penguin Books.

Sanden, Paul (2013). *Liveness in modern music: musicians, technology, and the perception of performance*. New York: Routledge.

Sexton, J. (2009). Digital music: production, distribution and consumption. In G. Creeber & R. Martin (eds.), *Digital cultures* (pp. 92–106). Berkshire: Open University Press.

The Beastie Boys (1998). *Intergalactic*. Capitol Records: Hello Nasty.

Unterstell, R. (2012). The power of music. *German Research*, 34(3), 20–22.

Section One

Live that survives

Live concerts and fan identity in the age of the Internet

1

R. Bennett

I notice that as the Net provides free or cheap versions of things, the "authentic experience"—the singular experience enjoyed without mediation—becomes more valuable.
Brian Eno (2011), "What I Notice"
Is the Internet Changing the Way You Think?

1.1 Introduction

I like all the different people
I like sticky everywhere
Look around, you bet I'll be there

The Breeders, "Saints"
Last Splash, *1993*

In an era where *virtual* experiences of live events are becoming increasingly sophisticated in terms of delivering real-time, shared experiences through screen-based Internet technologies (Bennett, 2012), the demand for *physically grounded* live music concerts is arguably stronger than ever (Holt, 2010). Looking past the digital hype that dominates the discussions of contemporary popular culture, this chapter stands as a reminder that *live* music—in the old-school sense of the term as a face-to-face meeting between artist and fan—still has a significant role to play. Pulling focus to an element of traditional musical culture that has survived and thrived, the digital revolution finds that the desire to participate in shared, corporeal musical experiences, in the form of live concerts, persists in a virtually enhanced present. Locating the discussion firmly on the fan experience in musical culture, this chapter searches for reasons why digitally savvy audiences actively seek out, celebrate, and pay for (at least partially) *un*mediated live music experiences.

Understanding the motivations and desires of live music audiences, who are integral players in live concert experiences, is crucial to understanding the role that nondigital elements of live music concerts play in a digitally evolving popular culture. As musicologist Marshall (2011) states, "an approach that sees meaning constructed by the listener emphasizes the active application of knowledge" (p. 159). This kind of fan-generated "knowledge" is explored in this chapter through the consideration of audience experience: namely, what meanings do musical audiences and fans derive from a live concert—and do these meaning take on a new significance in digital age? To answer these questions, I turn the spotlight away from what's happening on stage and shine it on the audience.

Henry Jenkins's (2006a,b) reflexive positioning of the fan as being crucial to the meaning (both individual and cultural), generated through popular culture texts, frames this analysis. The scope for interactive engagement with fan texts through multiple Internet platforms—particularity through social media—has altered the listener experience of live music, and music in general. It has also altered the way that live music is produced, promoted, and consumed. Concert audiences arguably have more power than ever before to influence the representation of live concerts, with the scope for publishing reviews, edited concert footage, images, and real-time commentary of live events in cyberspace for the broader musical fan base. Internet technology, particularly hand-held smartphone technology, and social media platforms mean that the "live concert" is no longer under the full control of artists, labels, or concert promoters; audiences and fans experiencing live concerts in person and online have unprecedented influence over the cultural meanings generated from musical events.

Internet technology creates an abundant space for everyday identity play and exploration; however, its global reach and changeability make it difficult to position a stable and secure sense of self online. The desire not only to explore the self but also to secure it is potentially why the significance of offline live concerts continues to grow, as does the capacity to engage with live concerts in real time, online. In 2003, when people were becoming comfortable communicating and spending large amounts of time in online spaces, cultural commentator David Boyle noticed a growing desire for slower, nonvirtual cultural activities: buying local, eating "slow" food, practicing yoga, and returning to "nature." He predicted that:

> *It is beginning to be clear that the dominant cultural force of the century ahead won't just be global and virtual, but a powerful interweaving of opposites—globalization and localization, virtual and real, with an advance guard constantly undermining what is packaged and drawing much of society along behind them.*
>
> *Boyle (2003), p. 4*

This paradoxical desire is demonstrated in live music culture today, while fans are active participants in virtual "live" experiences and there is a persistent hunger for real "live" experience both as "fuel" for the music economy and in the desire for the kind of multisensual and authentic experience that only face-to-face gigs can offer.

Examining the fan-generated meanings of musical experiences can offer only an incomplete and partial analysis. The effects of music are as affective as they are cognitive, and as such it is difficult to capture the full cultural significance of live music in words. Many aspects of audience desires for live music defy critical analysis, which in itself may be part of the reason why the live concert continues to be an important musical experience. Focusing on an element of the concert experience that can be explored—that of identity in a digital age—finds some answers for the question of their significance for fans. In his analysis of Springsteen fans, Cavicchi (1998, p. 37) argues that

> *for fans...a concert represents a powerful meeting of the various forces and people and ideas involved in their participation in musical life. The excitement of participation, the feeling of connection with Springsteen, the interaction of fans and other*

audience members, the rituals, the energy, the empowerment, the communal feeling, the evaluation, the discussion: together they enact the meaning of fandom. They shape and anchor fans' sense of who they are and where they belong.

Considering possible relationships between live music concerts and fan identity finds a partial rationale for the ever-present desire to attend live-music events in a shared physical space with artists and other fans, when boundaries between virtual and real are becoming increasingly harder to find. Locating this analysis in a nexus between fandom, live music, and digital technology, I draw upon Frith's (1987) early investigations into the social functions of popular music as being the *creation of identity, the organization of time and the management of feelings* (pp. 133–150). Such an analysis finds that the reciprocal musical exchange at an offline live concert—where artist and fan share not only the same time but also the same physical space—legitimates and authenticates the significance of musical experience and popular culture as identity markers in a digital age. In a context of countless virtual reproductions, communications, and simulations, face-to-face participation in a live concert audience has a renewed value for fan identity in terms of history, community, individuality, and experience.

1.2 Identity and live music

Extravert or introvert
Love is kind, and love hurts
Rebellion or conformity
What is my identity?

Pet Shop Boys, "Too Many People"
Alternative, 1995

The Pet Shop Boys' song title "Too Many People" captures the paradox of identity in late-capitalism. The search for things to identify with and connect to in a culture of abundance—a consumer-driven culture that in 1995, when the song was released, was about to expand rapidly with the uptake of the Internet—was characterized by an unprecedented level of agency and choice in terms of self-expression. Today, the global abundance of products, information, individuals, and communities available on the Internet exacerbates the notion that there are "too many people" to try to negotiate a secure place for the self. Popular psychologist Barry Schwartz (2004) describes this as a "paradox of choice," when in a late-capitalist culture of abundance, having too many options can be as paralyzing as having no choice at all. The abundance of identity markers available in an individualizing consumer-driven culture, combined with the ease with which local and national boundaries are crossed, both physically and virtually, means that the place of birth and family name are no longer the benchmarks of identity.

In a time characterized by liquid modernity (Bauman, 2000a) and accelerating change (Redhead, 2006), identity is a fluid and unstable construct: thus, it is often referred to as "process" (Bauman, 2001a), or a "performance" (Goffman, 1959), rather than a product. While external identity markers—such as ethnicity, age, gender, and class—limit the scope for identity formation, they no longer refer to a fixed, tangible, and easily understood identity or community. Instead, the concept of identity has moved beyond reference to a true and authentic singular "self" to relate to many possible "selves" that can be taken up and discarded, as contexts, roles, and situations change. While a fluid concept of identity can be viewed as a sign of freedom, agency, and liberation of the individual from constraints that are often beyond their control, it can also cause feelings of insecurity, isolation, and confusion (Bauman, 2000b) as individuals struggle to figure out where they "fit" in a globally connected and ever-changing worldview.

Zygmunt Bauman (2001b, p. 124) explains the transference of responsibility for identity from the social structure to the individual:

> *To put it in a nutshell, individualization consists in transforming human identity from a given into a task and charging the actors with the responsibility for performing that task.*

The individualization of identity has resulted in a paradox: on the one hand, identity is used to express an individual's difference from the "masses"; on the other hand, it is formed, validated, and secured in the groups and communities to which one belongs. Digital technology, and the Internet in particular, offers the ways for music fans to embrace the communal construction of identity with an abundance of fan communities (linked to almost any musical genre and artist) to identify *with* and *belong to*. For the live music fan, the Internet offers easy opportunities to connect with other fans and through a myriad of platforms including YouTube, Facebook, Twitter, fan forums, and official artist websites.

Being granted fast and easy access to communities to link one's identity to, coupled with the interactive ability to express an individual voice enabled through Web 2.0 and 3.0 interactivity, eases the paradoxical process of identity formation. However, the landscape of simulation and representation that constitute cyber-community interactions brings with it issues of authenticity and legitimacy, because it is difficult to ascertain whether community members are presenting an image that aligns with who they are offline. Additionally, the decoupling of time and space online, where real-time interactions can be accessed from virtually any local space across the globe, plus the permanent state of "renewal" brought about by constant upgrading of operating systems, coding languages, and interfaces, means that the experiences facilitated in "digital" spaces will make the fan experience difficult to memorialize and carry forward through time.

1.3 Live concerts and history

> *People used to make records*
> *As in a record of an event*
> *An event of people playing music in a room*
> *Now everything is cross marketing*

Its sunglasses and shoes
Or guns or drugs
You choose.

Ani Difranco, "Fuel"
Little Plastic Castle, 1998

The celebrated capabilities of digital information to be accessed anywhere and at any time—plus the rapid obsolescence of digital hardware and software—contribute to an uneasy relationship with the "past." Late-capitalist consumer culture is said to rely on "the suppression of historical and temporal perception" (Gilroy, 1987, p. 261), and Internet technology, with its ability to be accessed at any time from anywhere, is an ideal vehicle for identity formation based on continual consumption practices and constant change. However, a free-floating virtual identity is difficult to absorb into a body, occupying a fixed material space on the other side of the screen. Thus to create a tangible sense of identity that transfers from one side of the screen to the other, a linear narrative that tells a story of "who I am, where I have been, as well as where I want to be" is needed. Internet technology offers limited scope for writing a history for identity. Offline participation in a live concert is a way for someone to connect their fan-self to space and time. Thus, it provides individuals with the agency to write their own history, by positioning an aspect of their identity in a linear narrative of events. The live concert, as an unrepeatable moment in space and time, provides a music fan identity with historical legitimacy.

History is also significant for live music fans, in that it connects to a form of musical experience that existed prior to digital streaming and analog reproduction of concerts. Boyle argues that the ability to become virtually connected to an abundance of global networks has paradoxically transformed experiences of life offline into nostalgia for the local, the intimate, and the "real" (Boyle, 2003, p. 4). The desire to find ways to have an authentic musical experience through history—to mimic musical consumption as it might have been before the Internet—manifests in online subcultures such as Lucy Bennett's (2011) study into how a specific REM online fan group encouraged one another to resist technology and try to "restore the experience of listening to a new album as a singular event" (p. 748). This "inverted" form of cultural capital is evidence of a desire among online communities to connect with how people *used to* experience music. A popular memory of historical musical events, such as the now mythical "Summer of Love," informs cultural expectations of rock concerts and festivals. Kitts suggests that originally outdoor festivals such as Woodstock "strived to present images of freedom with their at least anticipated open spaces, seeming anarchy, and expected utopian communities" (Kitts, 2009, p. 718). The nostalgia for sharing in the experience of music as it was in an untainted vision of the past informs the contemporary live concert experience. The live music concert thus allows fans to feel connected to musical history, because it offers experiences that are similar to those that previous generations might have had. Being able to connect with a simpler, more authentic version of music experience that has survived through time offers a more secure place for identity than the elusive present does. Thus, the live concert can act to cement a place for the self in history, just as it evokes a sense of belonging to a community of live audiences that offers a sense of security because it has survived through time.

1.4 Live concerts and community

Who am I? AM crew to the death
Who am I? War crew to the death
Who am I? WA to the death
And I'm gonna represent till there's nothin' of me left

Drapht, "Who am I"
Who Am I, 2005

Music connects people to one another not only through a shared interest or hobby, but also through (imagined and real) emotional connections to particular songs, communities, and artists. The significance of others in the search for the self is significant; as Agger (2008) states, "identities are largely social products, formed in relation to others and how we think they view us" (p. 175). And Frith argues that popular music has (1987, p. 149). For music fans, the genres, artists, bands, DJs, songs, and albums in which people find meaning, thus, function as potential "places" through which one's identity can be positioned in relation to others: they act as tethers that hold at least parts of one's identity in place. The connections made through shared musical passions provide a sense of safety and security in the notion that there are groups of similar people who can provide the *feeling* of a community, if not the physical place for it.

The desire to feel as if one's identity is authentic and that communities of interest are more than simulations is satiated in offline interactions. Live concerts in material space complement participation in digital live music communities. The off-screen, physically and temporally bounded live concert experience helps to ground fan identity. The limitations and relative rigidity of the intersection between material space and linear time mean that identity is more easily verified offline. The prevalent use of programs, such as Photoshop to alter images, the factual "looseness" of Wikipedia, and the capacity for anonymity in online communications mean that it is difficult to ascertain whether any online object, person, or event is a true representation of its digital counterpart. It is in this context of virtual reproduction (which is discursively separated from *Real* Life) that David Boyle (2003) argues that the concept of authenticity has increased in significance, due to "the effect of an increasingly virtual world, where nothing is quite what it seems has led to a growing clamor for what is genuine and human" (Boyle, 2003, p. 12). The malleability of digital information means that Real Life offers a higher degree of authenticity than virtual space does. Thus, paradoxically, the digital format works to authenticate and elevate grounded, local, and face-to-face identifications enabled through attendance at a live concert, by offering less trustworthy virtual comparisons of community participation online.

The Internet has provided a forum not only for fans of particular artists but also for fans of the "live" music scene itself. Blogs and websites such as LIVE (2013), Join The Rukkus (2013), Live Fix (2013), Live Nation (2013), and Live Music Exchange (2013) are dedicated to the celebration of live concerts and performances. The emergence of an online discourse centered specifically on the live music form, regardless of the genre or artist, is evidence that the live concert experience is a persistent meaningful and revered musical form. As Sassen (2002, p. 368) explains,

> *Obversely, much of what happens in electronic space is deeply inflected by the cultures, the material practices, the imaginaries that take place outside of electronic space. Much of what we think of when it comes to cyberspace would lack any meaning or referents if we were to exclude the world outside cyberspace.*

The celebration of live music online maintains a reverence for "offline" engagement in the form. Without the referent of a physically bounded, embodied material concert as the primary object of the blog posts, discussions, and information sharing, these virtual communities are meaningless. Thus, when live music is the object of online engagement, discussions, reviews, file sharing, and sales, there is an implied physicality and materiality to the interactions, whether they occur online or offline. This material referent ensures that the offline concert experience is retained as the ideal: the authentic referent that online live music communities celebrate. Therefore, to consolidate full membership and link fan identity to a community focused on live music, there is an underlying requirement to have experience in engaging with the form offline.

The significance of offline attendance at a local live music event is enhanced through the global celebration of the experience in cyberspace. Thus, digital technology provides a vehicle for promoting, affirming, and elevating the importance of physical participation in a live concert, and ironically uses the on-screen community to encourage music fans to seek experiences off-screen. A blog post on Livemusicblog titled "Getting Ready for Gathering of the Vibes 2014 with Last Year's Photo/Highlights" is captioned with the statement: "my brain was flooded with memories from all of the times I moved into a temporary small town made of tents, stayed up until the sun came up and truly danced all of my cares away" (Lynne, 2013). In this celebration of live music, the "small town" analogy expresses the connection between identity and local community participation; the type of communal engagement imagined in a town carries very different connotations to the borderless cyberspace that comprises the community who congregate on the blog. The physical aspect of the music-festival-as-town metaphor is highlighted through the embodied reference to "dancing" cares away. Compared to the scope of the Internet, a relatively large music event is reconstituted as an embodied small town experience: a tangible local community with the power to alleviate worries of everyday life. The new positioning of local, grounded live events, as providing a point of difference to global, simulated live music experiences, impacts how the live concert functions as an identity marker, in terms of both community and individuality. The live concert has a renewed capacity for tethering identity to something fixed and tangible, because of its capacity to authenticate the self in ways that the Internet cannot.

An offline concert can evoke a sense of community that is reminiscent of romanticized community entanglements of a long-lost past. It provides tangible evidence that other fans are more than simulations, and demonstrates that online communities have a referent in "Real Life." Thus in many ways, the live concert experience fills "gaps" in cyberspace communities. Belonging to a crowd of like-minded people and sharing a physical, as well as a musical, experience lends a layer of tangibility and authenticity to community membership; a concert offers material evidence that there are "people like me" in the physical world, not just in the virtual one.

The live concert not only enhances a sense of belonging to a tangible community but also can increase a sense of intimacy and exclusivity. Membership to online music communities—and participation in live-streamed gigs—is theoretically open to anyone with an Internet connection, whereas an offline live concert community has a finite membership, limited to those with a ticket or to the capacity of a venue. This makes the offline live concert community an exclusive community, which in turn allows for a more specific positioning of the self among the masses. Being able to distinguish who one is *not* is as crucial to identity formation as the attempt to explain who one is. To *not* simply be one of the thousands of global fans who watch a live concert online, but to have the added status of also belonging to a local concert community (even if only for a very brief time) strengthens the connection to the event.

Online relationships can arguably be as psychologically significant as those forged offline and a deep sense of belonging and identity can be found in virtual communities. Boyle (2003, p. 60) argues that

> *there are two different categories of virtual real. There are manifestations where the end product is absolutely real—like time banks or online poetry. But there are also manifestations where what is delivered is real experience, in some ways, but the final product seem somehow to be compromised by the whole process.*

If a concert were streamed "live" to a virtual-only audience, then this would be an example of a virtual real experience. The virtual audience *is* the audience referent. However, when there is a dispersed online-only audience and an offline audience who share the same material space as the performers, the "liveness" of the concert is compromised for the audience members at home. In the live-streamed concert, the "real" live audience becomes part of the virtual performance of the concert. Offline audiences' cheers, tweets, posts, voices, and, sometimes, bodies are streamed along with the artists on stage—and they become the "real" audience, to the online audiences' virtual counterpart. Being connected to the concert referent deepens offline audiences' authenticity and downgrades online-only participation to a secondary "not quite as real" version.

When a live concert is streamed online, the local offline-concert community becomes the object of the online community's gaze. This, in turn, positions the offline live audience as an object of desire for those watching online, due to the intimacy and authenticity associated with a physically bounded community. When signifiers to the offline audience are streamed online, virtual audiences are made aware of their status as outsiders looking in at a *real* concert. The offline audience has a greater degree of agency over the communal concert experience. A real-life audience member can turn off their smartphone and focus on belonging and interacting within the exclusive and localized, physical concert community. Should an offline audience member choose to stay jacked-in and participate in live streaming and tweeting real-time concert updates, however, their experience will have the potential to be enhanced through access to the Internet. An offline audience member can perform their fandom to physical and virtual fan communities simultaneously, and thus experience and promote their "exclusive" local communal experience to an imagined global audience of fans.

1.5 Live concerts and the individual

In digital spaces, individuals sitting behind computer terminals have a large degree of control over their own identity construction. Digital space is, thus, constructed to suit the image that the individual wants to see and portray. However, as Kent (2012) argues, "a complete digital 'self' exists only for the person that it represents. Other individuals on the screen encounter fragments of digital identities, rather than experience it as a whole" (p. 245). Physically being at a concert, however, hands control of one's identity over to the gaze of others who have the power to reject, dismantle, or cement the identity (Goffman, 1959). At a live concert, the presence of other physical humans allows for multiple layers of authentication—including all five of the senses and a crowd full of witnesses—to legitimate the musical experience and membership of a community of people who share the same purpose for being in the space. Thus, attending a "live" concert allows individuals to perform a "whole self" that is aligned with the "complete digital self" that individuals display online, but that "whole individual" cannot be exposed to the online community for acceptance or rejection. An offline live concert experience, on the other hand, has scope for the performance of a more complex, nuanced, and synthesized identity. For the individual fan, the concert event conflates multiple aspects of the self and absorbs them into the body. Being at an event in person is a way to reconcile and synthesize fan fragments, allowing audiences to feel a more holistic connection with their fan identity and community.

Being able to present a sophisticated, complex, multilayered, convergent "self" to a music community is a significant aspect of the offline live concert experience. Prior to the Internet and its capacity to facilitate increasingly sophisticated forms of interactivity across global borders, the synthesis of fan and other identities was taken as a given, because there were very limited options available for real-time interactive community participation, outside of the face-to-face concert space. However, with virtual interactions becoming part of everyday life, the performance of the whole self becomes an unusual—and exceptional—experience. Participation in a live concert event not only demonstrates a fan's interest in a particular musical act, but also allows for a multilayered and synthesized performance of the individual self because of the scope for displaying multiple identity markers at once. In terms of the identity task, offline live audience members' outfits, hairstyles, perfume choices, make-up, movements, friendship group, dancing, singing, and even position in relation to the stage allow for an individually customized performance of fandom. The individual's body is not detached from the community, but immersed within it and authenticated by it.

Bringing the whole body to a live concert means that fans must present the less easily manipulated identity markers, such as age, race, gender, and class to the fan community, as well as the markers under the individual's control. Adding this layer of vulnerability to the performance of the self and exposing parts of the identity that are out of one's control can enhance the feelings of acceptance and belonging—if these immovable markers are embraced as part of the crowd and community too. Thus, when compared to the fragmented experience of digital identity formed through partial engagement in multiple platforms and fan communities, individual identity at a concert is a synthesized whole. In material space, fans bring more to the concert than just their fandom; a whole self is on display, ready for acceptance or rejection from the crowd.

Digital technology works to enhance identity building through live concert experience by creating a new significance for face-to-face participation in music events. The intersection between Internet technology and live concert attendance can elevate the status of the digital fan to an elite group of "special" fans who have had a unique, one-off experience with an artist. Somewhat ironically, access to digital smartphone technology while at a gig enables the individual fan to promote their "authentic" offline musical experiences to a global fan community, rather than a few analog friends.

The reciprocal interaction between digital technology and live concerts is that recorded evidence that "one was there *then*" is easily collected via smartphone technology. This elevates fan status, in that interactive digital technology allows fans to publicize their attendance at an unrepeatable, one-off, exclusive event online. Even if nobody views live concert footage uploaded to YouTube, fan sites or Tumblr pages, individuals have a *potential* audience of millions for their evidence of attendance at a one-off live event. When the small local audience engaged in a physical live concert is compared to the massive global audience that could engage in a live-streamed version of the same event, the offline live concert becomes a more exclusive and "boutique" experience of fandom and a historical marker etched into the individual fan, distinguishing them from all who were not physically present. Attending a one-off live gig thus elevates a fan to a different status in the digital fan community, as they have accessed an exclusive fan space that cannot be reproduced, but which can be repeated multiple times online.

The capacity to upload "selfies" with artists or videos means that audience members can illustrate how physically close and intimate they get to artists at a live gig. Digital technology provided one Beyoncé fan with global fame after an Internet "selfie" taken a Beyoncé concert in Australia went viral. The initial story was that Beyoncé spontaneously photo bombed an audience member's selfie in the middle of a live concert in Sydney. The "selfie" image, uploaded to the 15-year-old Valentina's Tumblr page (N-uumb, 2014), and a gif created out of additional amateur footage that filmed the "photo bomb" moment were posted on news sites (The Daily Mail, 2013; The West Australian, 2013) and weblogs (Kelly, 2013; Ortiz, 2013; The Buzz, 2013; Weber, 2013) across the globe. Valentina's image became, momentarily, famous due to the capacity of smartphone technology and social media (Duivestine, 2013) to promote an individual fan moment between her and Beyoncé at a live concert. It was later found that the fan had actually asked Beyoncé for the photo, but this new storyline and Valentina's admission that in "truth" she asked Beyoncé for the photo kept Valentina in the news media cycle for longer. In this case, social media technology, plus the authenticity granted to face-to-face live performances, elevated the visibility of an individual fan for a prolonged period, simply through sharing a live moment with a famous music artist online. Prior to Web 3.0 technology, this intimate fan-artist moment would have been a locally contained event (potentially raising envy only among other concert goers and maybe a close group of friends). However, due to the globally networked aspects of identities that can be performed online, an individual was fleetingly raised to the status of a celebrity.

The intersections between online celebrations of live music, offline live music moments, and hand-held digital technologies are formed through an intricate and complex weaving of virtual and real. Offline, Beyoncé was thought to have inserted herself in a fan's digitally captured "selfie" and arguably the moment would not have happened had the fan not had a digital camera phone in her hand. Paradoxically, this moment became famous because while so many have the chance to follow Beyoncé's Instagram photos and tweets, the odds of meeting her in person appear greater. The Internet, thus, intensifies fan desires for offline interaction with music artists in the collective reverence for local, live music events. To be noticed and plucked out of a crowd of people and placed onstage means that the individual is guaranteed a huge audience for their identity—their difference from the rest is marked for as long as they are on stage. However, the conflation between the live concert and fan technology transformed a relatively small and banal moment in the audience, which previously might have only stayed with one individual—and perhaps a handful of audience members next to her—into a global news story, and the individual was granted an audience of global proportions that lasted well beyond the fixed time of the concert.

1.6 Conclusion

Digital communication technology is pushing the boundaries of the live music experience, especially with its potential for real-time interactions between concert-goers and other fans to engage with concerts as they are happening. While it is apparent that new kinds of live musical experiences are being facilitated in digital places, the face-to-face concert experience appears far from redundant in a digital age. The restructuring of the cultural significance of the live concert for audiences has been shaped by increasingly social, mobile, and interactive digital technologies—particularly in terms of writing musical consumption into narratives about and for the self. Holt (2010, p. 255) argues,

> *The restructuring of the live music economy is to a high degree related to factors beyond the music itself, especially the qualities of live experience, but also the social conditions of media and capitalism and postmodern narratives of self-realization through cultural consumptions.*

The process of finding the self through music is a search for meaning in a market-saturated, consumer-driven, and mass-produced world. Fandom provides an avenue through which to explore, express, share, and validate musical meaning. Grossberg (1992) states that "the very notion of a fan assumes the close relationship between identity and caring: it assumes that what matters—what has authority—is the appropriate ground for a stable identity" (p. 60). Physical participation in a live concert in real time and material space helps to stabilize fan identity in ways that the nonlinear, nested, and fragmented configuration of cyberspace(s) cannot. For live music fans, the face-to-face concert lends a layer of authenticity to musical enjoyment as an identity marker, due to its relative fixity and trustworthiness, when compared to the fluid and easily manipulated digital landscape.

Experiencing live music as it was in a predigital past offers a brief reprieve from the social conditions brought about by digitally infused consumer culture. The live concert as an unrepeatable, exclusive event, grounded in time and space, envelops fan identity in a local and tangible community, of which performers on stage are a part. For the individual fan, the offline live concert not only offers intimate access to performers but also provides an audience for a live performance for multiple aspects of the self beyond the screen. Being able to present multiple identity markers simultaneously and thus perform a consolidated sense of embodied self to a physical local community has become a comparatively unusual experience in a digital age.

Exploring how offline live music concerts function in terms of shaping identity in the age of the Internet finds that the desire to share in a reciprocal musical exchange where artist and fan share not only the same time but also the same physical space is ever-present and takes on a potentially greater significance in a musical culture where full and immersive participation is often interrupted by the invisible, yet tangible, barrier of a digital screen.

References

Agger, B. (2008). *The virtual self: A contemporary sociology*. Carlton: Blackwell Publishing.

Bauman, Z. (2000a). *Liquid modernity*. Cambridge: Polity Press.

Bauman, Z. (2000b). *Community: Seeking safety in an insecure world*. Cambridge: Polity Press.

Bauman, Z. (2001a). Identity in the globalizing world. *Social Anthropology*, 9(2), 121–129.

Bauman, Z. (2001b). *The individualized society*. Cambridge: Polity Press.

Bennett, L. (2011). Music fandom online: R.E.M. fans in pursuit of the ultimate first listen. *New Media and Society*, 14(5), 748–763.

Bennett, L. (2012). Patterns of listening through social media: online fan engagement with the live music experience. *Social Semiotics*, 22(5), 545–557.

Boyle, D. (2003). *Authenticity: Brands, fakes, spin and the lust for real life*. London: Flamingo.

Cavicchi, D. (1998). *Tramps like us: Music and meaning amongst Springsteen fans*. Oxford: Oxford University Press.

Duivestine, S. (2013). *Fan makes #selfie with Beyonce*. Retrieved from https://www.youtube.com/watch?v=_e8oc4CikvU.

Eno, B. (2011). What I notice. In J. Brockman (Ed.), *Is the Internet changing the way you think?* (pp. 27). New York: Harper Perennial.

Frith, S. (1987). Towards an aesthetic of popular music. In R. Leppert & S. McClary (Eds), *Music and society: The politics of composition, performance and reception* (pp. 133–150). Cambridge: Cambridge University Press.

Gilroy, P. (1987). *There ain't no black in the Union Jack*. New York: Routledge.

Goffman, E. (1959). *The presentation of the self in everyday life*. London: Anchor Books.

Grossberg, L. (1992). Is there a fan in the house?: The affective sensibilities of fandom. In L. A. Lewis (Ed.), *The adoring audience: Fan culture and popular media* (pp. 50–65). London: Routledge.

Holt, F. (2010). The economy of live music in the digital age. *European Journal of Cultural Studies*, 13(2), 243–261.

Jenkins, H. (2006a). *Convergence culture: Where old and new media collide*. New York: New York University Press.

Jenkins, H. (2006b). *Fans, bloggers and gamers: Exploring participatory cultures*. New York: New York University Press.

Join The Rukkus (2013). *Join the Rukkus*. http://rukkus.com/blog.

Kelly, S. (2013). Beyonce 'Photobomb' is the greatest selfie of all time. *Mashable*. Retrieved from http://mashable.com/2013/10/29/beyonce-photobombed-selfie.

Kent, M. (2012). When community becomes a commodity. In T. Brabazon (Ed.), *Digital dialogues and community 2.0: After avatars, trolls and puppets* (pp. 244–252). Cambridge: Chandos Publishing.

Kitts, T. (2009). Documenting, creating, and interpreting moments of definition: Monterey Pop, Woodstock, and Gimme Shelter. *The Journal of Popular Culture*, 42(4), 715–732.

LIVE (2013). *LIVE*. Retrieved from www.livemusicblog.com.

Live Fix (2013). *Live fix*. http://christophercatania.com.

Live Music Exchange (2013). *Live music exchange*. http://livemusicexchange.org.

Live Nation (2013). *Live nation*. Retrieved from http://www.livenation.com.au.

Lynne, D. (2013). *Getting ready for the gathering of the vibes*. Retrieved from http://livemusicblog.com/2014/05/29/getting-ready-for-gathering-of-the-vibes-2014-with-last-years-photohighlights.

Marshall, L. (2011). The sociology of popular music, interdisciplinarity and aesthetic autonomy. *The British Journal of Sociology*, 62(1), 154–174.

N-uumb (2014). *Valentina*. Retrieved from http://n-uumb.tumblr.com/post/65314514772/are-you-the-girl-who-was-at-the-melbourne-show-and.

Ortiz, E. (2013). *Beyoncé photobombs fan taking a selfie at concert in Australia*. Retrieved from http://www.complex.com/music/2013/10/beyonce-photobombs-fan-selfie-picture.

Redhead, S. (2006). The art of the accident: Paul Virilio and accelerated modernity. *Fast Capitalism*, 2(1), 1–2.

Sassen, S. (2002). Towards a sociology of information technology. *Current Sociology*, 50(3), 365–388.

Schwartz, B. (2004). *The paradox of choice: Why more is less*. New York: Harper Collins.

The Buzz (2013). Beyonce photobombs fan's selfie. *The Buzz*. Retrieved from http://thebuzzcincy.newsone.com/1671375/am-buzz-beyonce-photobombs-fans-selfie.

The Daily Mail (2013). Best photobomb ever! Beyonce delights fan as she stops singing to join her selfie midway through concert. *The Daily Mail*. Retrieved from http://www.dailymail.co.uk/tvshowbiz/article-2479008/Best-photobomb-Beyonce-delights-fan-stops-singing-join-selfie-midway-concert.html.

The West Australian (2013). Beyonce photobombs Oz fan's selfie. *The West Australian*. Retrieved from https://au.news.yahoo.com/thewest/entertainment/access-all-areas/a/19603541/beyonce-photobombs-oz-fans-selfie.

Weber, L. (2013). What happens when Beyoncé photo-bombs your selfie. *Vulture*. Retrieved from http://www.vulture.com/2013/10/what-happens-when-beyonce-photobombs-your-selfie.html.

Aura, iteration, and action: digital technology and the jouissance of live music

2

T. Harper

As predicted by Marx in *Grundrisse*, in an effort to stimulate production and consumption, capitalism is annihilating space by time (Marx, 1973, p. 538). As a society we have tended to embrace this annihilation, as technology allows us to become closer to each other and the world—giving us a privileged perspective on everything from global sporting events to the intimate appearance of a lover on the other side of the world. While the benefits of this annihilation are seemingly endless, there are a few instances where local culture seems to be resistant to such mediation. One of these instances is live music, where there is a sense that "being there" means something much more than simply "being there [online]." I would argue that what is missing from online live performance is an experience of "jouissance," a feeling of pleasure that is experienced through the incommensurable uniqueness of the event. This chapter is an attempt to explore what digital technology will struggle to capture about experiencing music live.[1]

2.1 The territory: arguments about the technological mediation of cultural production

The case against digital technology as a medium for live music is probably best established by Adorno and Horkheimer's infamous essay "The Culture Industry: Enlightenment as Mass Deception" (Adorno & Horkheimer, 1997). Developing directly out of a Marxist appraisal of the role of entertainment in an industrialized age of cultural production, "The Culture Industry" explains how capital spreads its tendrils through culture to ensure that the underclass remains productive and consumptive. A number of assertions made by Adorno and Horkheimer seem particularly prescient when thinking about attempts to "mediate" live music through digital technology. For instance, Adorno and Horkheimer insist that:

[1] The structure of the chapter mirrors the iterative form of Miles Davis's jazz composition. It will first examine the "territory" of arguments about how mechanical reproduction and distribution affects cultural production before embarking upon an "expedition" of personal reflections on live music experiences which could prove difficult to reproduce online. As the chapter makes an argument about the experiential qualities of music, there is also a YouTube playlist which features musicians mentioned throughout the chapter in the order they are mentioned. The playlist can be found at http://www.youtube.com/playlist?list=PLTS51BV9daZYr48n-HxZXyAr1BEPzzr1T

The Digital Evolution of Live Music

> *Amusement under late capitalism is the prolongation of work. It is sought after as an escape from the mechanised work process, and to recruit strength in order to be able to cope with it again. But at the same time mechanisation has such power over a man's leisure and happiness, and so profoundly determines the manufacture of amusement goods, that his experiences are inevitably after-images of the work process itself.*
>
> *Adorno & Horkheimer (1997), p. 137*

So, whereas once people went to massive buildings to work, placed in largely anonymous positions and asked to do nothing more than perform highly coded action, these days work increasingly involves sitting with a computer, clicking away, switching between windows and roles. The transition from live music as a stadium experience to a screened experience can be understood to reflect this change in working experiences. The prevalence of communication technology means that matter matters less, as a result of the collapse of space and time.

The concern that Adorno and Horkheimer have with such work-like amusement is that it stymies any recognition of different spheres of action, of other ways of being. Instead of us enjoying something contrary in our leisure time, we experience more sameness, and thus "both escape and elopement are predesigned to lead back to the starting point. Pleasure promotes the resignation which it ought to help to forget" (Adorno & Horkheimer, 1997, p. 142). The loss of identity that characterized the age of mechanical reproduction can be understood to be reflected in the somewhat anonymous reception of live stadium music, whereas the particular anomie engendered by personal computing is reflected in the isolation of receiving live music digitally. In both cases, work and play can be understood to ameliorate revolutionary impulses and restrict the possibilities of new experiences and connections.

On the other hand, separated by both space and time from the writers of "The Culture Industry," we can witness Henry Jenkins' response to the culture industry and its relation to digital culture in his work on convergence culture (Jenkins, 2006). In this piece, Jenkins takes a far more positive view of digital mediation and its effects on cultural production. Using quilt making as an example, he compares localized "folk" production with industrialized and then digitized production. He emphasizes that folk production occurs organically within a community, using the tools at hand and cultural knowledge, whereas industrialized production is dislocated, involving isolated processes, productions, and areas of expertise. He concludes with the point that digital cultures allow for the best of all worlds. They expand the accessibility of cultural production and allow for the dissemination of otherwise local cultures and practices and foster broad connections between cultures. Jenkins uses the "digital quilt" of communimage (see http://www.communimage.ch) as an example of such production. On this site, participants from around the world have collaboratively added a patchwork of images to form a pastiche image which constantly evolves and grows. The components of this quilt don't necessarily speak to each other through an overarching principle aside from participation; the original "cult value" of the various images is overwhelmed by the normative value of the concept of egalitarian participation.

Jenkins is essentially suggesting that digital technology allows us to recover the humanity of culture by becoming more participatory. Hence Jenkins provides an antithesis to Adorno and Horkheimer's paranoia about the problems with mediating culture through technology. Following Mark Poster's explanation that "the magic of the internet is that it puts cultural acts … in the hands of all participants" (Poster, 1997, p. 224), Jenkins' work suggests that the digitization of live music may actually provide for a better experience than industrialized live music because the assembled shared experience is necessarily emergent—a synthesis of the participating cultures.

But while we might follow Jenkins in understanding that participation undermines the stultifying effects of industrially mediated culture, what is the effect of inserting a technological distance between participants? Lying somewhere between Adorno and Horkheimer's pessimistic view and Jenkins' optimistic one lies the perspective of Walter Benjamin in his essay "The work of art in the age of mechanical reproduction" (Benjamin, 1936). In this piece, Benjamin identifies some of the more immanent issues with mediating live performance through technology. He broadly identifies that the mechanical reproduction of any artistic event deprives the artist of an audience, as it introduces a distance between them. This distancing has a number of positive and negative effects, which establish the framework for critiquing the effect of digital technology on musical performance.

On the positive side, Benjamin identifies that this distance allows the "cult value" of the art to recede into the background. As Jenkins identified almost 70 years later, the process of mediation means that the aesthetic experience loses some of its implied meaning and becomes more open to interpretation. Benjamin identified that the process of reproduction also opens up more possible facets for audience control of the art. The art can simply reach more places and, once it is there, it can be examined in detail by a wide audience and represents an elevation of the position of the audience member in the relationship between artist and audience. All of a sudden, the audience member has some control, and Benjamin—particularly in his afterword inspired by fascistic use of mass media—was particularly careful to emphasize that inviting such participation—and establishing some egalitarianism in production—was by far the best outcome of mechanical reproduction.

However, all these gains did not come without losses. With the greater distance between the artist and the audience, the artist lost the opportunity to respond to the audience. Whether this means that the artist lacks the feeling of appreciation generated by art, or lacks the opportunity to respond iteratively to the moment of reception, the meaning is the same; there is the loss of a sense of occasion. With this comes the sense that the artist's range of action is somehow constrained, as is the audience's opportunity to affect the artist. With the elevation of the art as the thing to be reproduced, rather than the artist or audience, Benjamin articulated that under mechanical reproduction, the priority is that the audience absorbs the art, rather than the art (or artist) absorbing the audience (Benjamin, 1936, p. 13).

What damage does this do to experience? The importance of iteration and action, response and relatedness for artists and audiences cannot be stressed enough. To understand this, it is helpful to turn toward Benjamin's friend Hannah Arendt, who bases her political philosophy around the importance of action. Arendt strongly believes in agency, the ability for individuals to have a radical, original impact upon the world. However, agency is delicate and only emerges under conditions of immanence, which must emerge in the space "between past and future" (Merchart, 2006), resisting the determinacy of passivity, knowledge, and technology. Action will "disclose the agent in the act," allowing the actor an expression of identity (Arendt, 1958, p. 183). Importantly, this expression is not entirely determined by the "cult value" of the past, nor is it entirely separate from what has happened before. Similarly, the action is not entirely predetermined by what is to happen in the future; there is space in action for iteration. That is for response to events as they happen, for the change of plans, the interaction of others; action cannot simply be fabrication (poiesis), it happens here and now (Arendt, 1967, p. 475). For Arendt, this suggests that representative democracy can never fulfill the important function of valorization that individual sovereignty otherwise demands. In relation to live music, this suggests that any attempt to digitally replicate live music simply must allow for interaction between the artist and audience to protect the possibility of the validation that this provides for the artist, the audience, and the art.

The various attempts to promote live digital music seem to indicate an awareness of the need to provide the space for iteration and action via the technology. Anyone who has seen the quiet isolation of most artists without an audience can understand the anomie that this develops. Among the purveyors of live digital music there is an overwhelming conviction that the thing that matters in this situation is audience feedback. As live music webcasting director Marc Scapa notes, "Instant participatory engagement is becoming key to the consumption of online entertainment, and the only way to do that is to make sure it's live … The key is participation in live events. That's something you can't do with a television broadcast" (Van Buskirk, 2009). As such, entertainment companies are focusing on developing technology that will allow a process of instant dissemination and feedback during "digital live music events." The goal here is to allow the artist not only to see the audience in real time but also to hear the audience, through a series of webcams and personal microphones. The feeling of real-time participation is seen to be the key to valorizing the live music experience.

Arendt's description of humanizing action, that the action must take place *now*, "between past and future," is important; however, so is the fact that action takes place *here*, within a physical place. This is because, she argues, there are a number of intangible aspects to physical presence that allow for the unsolicited interruptions, interventions, and revelations that vastly deepen our experiences (Arendt, 1958, p. 183). Benjamin best describes this collection of intangible aspects as the "aura" of the original—that aspect of the physical presence that can only be experienced through being there. As Benjamin says, "Even the most perfect reproduction of a work of art is lacking in one element: its presence in time and space, its unique existence at the place where it happens to be" (Benjamin, 1936, p. 3). It is inherently difficult to describe intangibles, which is possibly the thing that also makes them hard to reproduce mechanically. Nevertheless, what follows is an attempt to articulate what an "aura" represents.

I have a coffee mug with Pablo Picasso's *Guernica* printed upon it. This mechanical reproduction of the *Guernica* (or what I call "The Guernicup") is a poor reminiscence of what it is to see the massive and important piece of art in all its majesty. The original hangs as the centerpiece of the Museo Reina Sofia in Madrid, and at more than 21 m^2 provides an overwhelming physical experience for its audience. Beyond its sheer size, the canvas carries cracks and marks that have been accumulated over years of the painting being toured around the United States and Britain as a way to raise funds for the fight against fascism. My personal experience of seeing the *Guernica*—the original—was shaped by a particularly breathless endorsement of the power of the experience by my high school literature teacher, Mr. Rayner. It took me a further 20 years after hearing about the *Guernica* to actually come to see it, and the process of achieving the viewing, of traveling to Madrid, lining up outside the museum, and then standing there, agape, with maybe 50 other people in the room, was as important to the experience as the art itself. The space of the experience is as important as the time.

The aura of something, according to Benjamin, is about this spatial authenticity, and in another important way, it is also about personal distance and relativity. One needs to be proximate to something to experience its aura, not only to gather its sense of where it is in relation to "things," but also to establish the relation of the art to you. That is, to feel the art gazing back at you, imparting the understanding that your presence has added to the meaning of the work. While the use of webcams, monitors, and microphones can approximate the appearance and the sound of an artist or an audience, it cannot completely eliminate the distance between the two, and thus technological mediation will always inhibit the intimacy required to "feel" an aura.

The notion of auras, intimacy, and feeling brings me to the final part of the territory of this chapter, which is my suggestion that the crucial element of the live music experience is that the combination of action, iteration, and aura could be thought of as "jouissance," a concept that helps to define what digital or mechanical reproduction is unable to replicate. Jouissance is a deep, unrelatable sense of pleasure, such as that experienced during orgasm. While jouissance has been interpreted and used in a number of interesting ways, I would like to start with Barthes' use of the term in *The Pleasure of the Text* (Barthes, 1975). Here Barthes opposes the "generic" pleasure, which is a well-ordered response on behalf of the reader, to the jouissance experienced through a challenging read, a versatile text that undermines the dominant reading or interpretation. While generic pleasure results from the repetition of established codes and readings, jouissance is experienced when such structures are fractured and become active and inherent in the moment of interpretation. The iterative nature of the "unexpected" can be further explained through Lacan's use of the term, where "jouissance" is seen to refer to an "excess" of pleasure. According to Lacan, we have an inherent drive to experience jouissance, and yet our psyches also occupy themselves with preventing such an "excess" of pleasure (Lacan, 1992). As a result, we experience jouissance not necessarily because of what we planned to do, but only because of a culmination of interactions that we could (or would) not manufacture or predict. Deleuze rails against Lacan's description of jouissance as always implying an excess, insisting that this notion of lack is precipitated by an Oedipal, masculine imagination (Deleuze, 2001) and elsewhere insists that pleasure should be experienced through multiple, symbiotic, and harmonic connections (Deleuze & Guattari, 1987). Following on from this, Helene Cixous celebrates jouissance as an intense physical, spiritual, and mental experience that is a type of mystical communion realizable in moments of multiple orgasm (Cixous & Clement, 1975). What these interpretations share is an understanding that jouissance is immanent, it is ecstatic, it cannot be maintained, and it cannot actually be prescribed, but nevertheless will always be sought after. As both a term and an experience, it is difficult to describe but very clearly experienced.

The major problem that digital attempts to capture live music face is that they restrict the possibilities of the unexpected, expansive, and iterative experience. Physical experiences present peculiar opportunities for interactions, accidents, and revelations which digital technology will always struggle to replicate. Much of this is due to the intransigence of the characteristics of auras and the experience of jouissance, which are beyond technical reproduction. While it is clear that attempts to digitize live music are equally attempts to completely annihilate space, following Benjamin, there are reasons to believe that this may not be entirely possible. What follows is my attempt to account for what may be missing from digital experience through a series of personal tales about my own engagements with live music and digital technology.

2.2 The expedition: experiences of jouissance through live music

I am a lover of music, and indeed, for much of my life, my ultimate goal was to experience my favorite bands and musicians live. Here I shall endeavor to recount some of these events as a way of providing examples of the peculiar jouissance of live music and reflect on the attempts to capture that feeling digitally. Jouissance is in some sense incommensurable—it cannot be explained or described—but what I hope to do is provide some guidelines about some of the ecstasies that live music does produce and what digital technology needs to capture to replicate these experiences.

I shall start with Depeche Mode's *Devotional* Tour, which visited Perth in early 1994. The concert itself was awe-inspiring in terms of the raw energy displayed by lead singer David Gahn who, rumored to be on a opiate binge at the time, was the personification of an artist who had completely invested himself in the performance. His exalted performance got the crowd on their feet and in the surge I was able to squirm my way to the first few rows of the crowd. There I could feel the sweat and the heat emanating from the band, not to mention the press of the crowd around me, who were moving and singing while completely absorbed by the moment. The band fed off the energy of the crowd, who were in turn inspired by the passion of the band. My nearest approximation of this experience of this semimystic, trance-like experience would be a kecak dance in Bali, Indonesia, where a group of dancers sit before an "actor," chanting and waving their arms in unison throughout the performance. This chanting, seemingly provided by the spectators, creates a sense of a "plateau" of energy which complements and reflects the performance at the center. Called a "trance dance," the prevalence of such cultural forms is one of the more pertinent reminders of the complete visceral saturation that happens during a live performance and of the importance of feeling absorbed by the art.

Aside from the performance itself, there was another aspect of the Depeche Mode concert which would be difficult to replicate online—the ritual of the acquisition of the tickets. This was before event tickets were predominantly sold online and so, with time on our hands and enthusiasm in our hearts, some friends and I actually queued outside the venue for some 36 hours to acquire the best possible seats. This not only allowed for significant fun "down time" for me and my friends but also introduced us to a number of other people with whom we bonded over our love of the band. During the night we took turns waiting in line, returning to houses to equip with more supplies and generally developing a sense of community. This stood us in good stead when sales finally opened, as we were able to collectively identify and defend those of us who had stayed in line against latecomers who sought to jump the queue. Again, when we finally got to the concert, seeing our newly made friends added to the joy of the experience.

In 1993, I had to be in a physical queue for Depeche Mode tickets to be able to identify another person as a Depeche Mode fan, or we needed to display some other cultural signifier—a tour shirt, or maybe a Martin Gore-inspired sequined shorts and perm. With the advent of digital technology and particularly social media, it is far, far easier to identify others with shared interests. According to Jenkins' theories, this should allow for a greater participation in communities and, of course, greater access to culture. These points are hard to argue against as, when it comes to access, digital technology, like mechanical reproduction, brings the art to more people, in more places, in a way that has to be considered essentially emancipatory. Nevertheless, there was something about the physical presence of those in the line which created an impetus toward becoming friends and forming a community—a certain imperative of physical coexistence: eating, sleeping, pissing—that is not found online.

Another aspect of seeing a band live can be found in the uniqueness of the experience—that is, having a sense of occasion derived from the fact that this is a unique event which will never be experienced by anyone else in a different space or a different time. This is perhaps the most selfish of motives, but can be understood by anyone who has ever felt as though the music was being played just for them, that this moment would never be replicated or could never be captured. Typified in arguments about knowing a band before they were cool, I reflect on this through Radiohead. I've seen Radiohead on three occasions. The last time was in a crowd of about 20,000 screaming and adoring fans in a city on the other side of the world, whereas the first time was with about 200 people in a club only 3 km from my house. It wasn't necessarily that Radiohead were unheard of when they toured Australia in 1994, but they were a relatively small band with one hit single "Creep," so much of the small audience left shortly after they'd played their hit. I, on the other hand, had their first album and a couple of bootlegs, and had concluded that they were talented. As a result, in that first concert it was only a handful of us watching Radiohead in a largely empty venue. While I enjoyed seeing them twice more, there is an element of that first experience which takes pride of place in my memory of them because the experience was relatively unique, something I got to enjoy while at least 19,800 other people never did.

Clearly having a unique digital music experience is possible but, in reality, the entire digital economy is about making access more universal, rather than restricting access. Not only is any performance now able to be produced for a digital audience and distributed ad infinitum; the enjoyment of live performance is somewhat undermined by the perpetual recording and inscription of the events during the events themselves. In this instance, the opportunities for iterative and active engagement in the process are elided by a desire to be seen and understood to have been witness to the "original" by transposing it to a copy. I experienced this recently at a Ben Folds Five reunion tour, when my wife was so busy recording her favorite song on her smartphone that she missed the chance to dance to her favorite song (and this after she sneered at a couple who she saw updating their Facebook page earlier in the evening!). This is possibly a breaking point for the digital/live music debate, where rather than complementing each other they can be seen as antagonistic cultures; the former values endless constant access, the latter authenticity and visceral engagement.

Another possibility inherent to live music is the possibility of the unexpected event or tangential experience. As described by Barthes and Lacan, one of the elements of jouissance is its sense of excess, of being beyond a plan or prescription. So it was with me that when I went to Glastonbury in 2005, one of my highlights came from not what I had prepared for but from a couple of random interactions. On the first day, in front of John Butler Trio, I bumped into an old friend among a crowd of about 60,000. Then, after deciding to take a break from the music to attend a community discussion about political activism, I was thrilled to find one of my musical heroes Billy Bragg leading the discussion. With about 10 others attending, this was my equivalent of walking into the sermon on the mount.

Digital technology certainly enables a number of connections to take place, with the possibility being opened up that instead of choosing to either see Kaiser Chiefs on the pyramid stage OR attend the politics and activism discussion, I could digitally do both at the same time, while chatting to friends on social media and writing an e-mail to Billy Bragg. This would be relatively easy to organize, and I could also manage these experiences around my own time and the other important events in my life. However, in making these experiences expected and predictable, the connections themselves don't replicate the feeling of euphoria, uniqueness, and jouissance engendered by the emergent, situated experience. Yes, you could be thrilled by a pop-up conversation from a messaging service, but such interactions remain far more homogenized and controllable than a live experience.

There are also broader experiences associated with crowd behavior that I feel are simply impossible to reproduce digitally. I was witness to one such event watching Cypress Hill at the Belmont Racecourse in Perth in 2003. During the set the entire crowd started to cheer as some interlopers sprinted across the racecourse being chased by security. As one we expressed our encouragement, reservations, and then celebration as the two of them made the security fence and were able to haul themselves over into the crowd, narrowly escaping the clutching grasps of the security staff on the outside of the event. For the audience, this act of subversion perfectly echoed and complemented the "aura" of the Cypress Hill performance. While it is clear that online audiences have a whole raft of options to engage in activism and communal expression when online, how exposed are they to universal experiences which may not be recorded on camera but remain fundamental to a live music experience? Some attempts to capture these "broader experiences" have been made, significantly by the Beastie Boys who filmed their 2005 tour by handing out 50 digital cameras to selected audience members to record "their take" on a single concert (Yauch, 2006). The result is hugely interesting, with shots from various positions in the audience of the band and includes shots of crowd members "making out," visions of celebrities in the audience, and even footage of one of the camera operators visiting the toilet. All of this does add up to an experience that is close to "being there," and possibly in terms of access to various perspectives, backstage, and celebrities, even better than the real thing.

In their mysterious ways, U2 have pioneered the live broadcast of music via their "U2ube" initiative, and they provide some counterbalance to what might otherwise be considered a one-sided account of live digital music. Being a fan and seeing the video of U2's *360* tour, as well as physically attending the live show, I can attest to the fact that the former was almost as good as the latter. With something like 40,000 people in the venue, the live experience was mostly mediated by the massive screens suspended above the artists and the performance itself was immensely similar to the one found on the video. Hence, I can see the argument that in some situations and given certain parameters, watching a band via digital technology can emulate the experience of being there. U2's live digital broadcasting of their concerts is a real bonus for those of us who live "off the beaten track" of stadium tours. Nevertheless, I find this U2 experience to be an exception that proves the rule.

Conversely, the best possible expression I can muster of all the glory of "cult value" and aura is my attendance at the REM *Monster* tour, which started in my home town in 1995. I was absolutely smitten by the mixture of mystique, intelligence, and fun that REM represented and thus I found myself again queuing overnight, twice, to get the best possible tickets for their first two shows. Following a familiar process of ticket queue bonding and co-opting ticket ordering, I found myself on the night surrounded by friends who also loved the band. Not only this, but sitting front and center, I was directly in front of Michael Stipe as he made his way through the set. This meant there was opportunity for interaction, an odd smile or a nod between myself and Michael. But after he sung "Country Feedback," a maudlin and beautiful song which I held close to my heart at the time for reasons I thought only I knew, Michael reached down to the audience and passed me the lyric sheet. Why did he choose me? How could he know that it was simply the most meaningful thing he could have done? Benjamin (and Arendt) would argue that aura played a part. I have kept the sheet to this day, a reminder of how close I came to greatness, a manifestation of an ideal in physical form. Part of me has lost the misty-eyed attitude that holds musicians as purveyors of everything good in the world; however, I also get the sheet out every now and again to remind myself that amazing things really happen, that what is incredible and romantic can also be physically manifest and real.

My final example is one that shows how a large number of these aspects conspire to form an experience that I feel cannot be replicated digitally. In 1996 I went hitch-hiking around Britain and Ireland. I was fortunate enough, in the process, to get a lift from a music producer. Discussing his most recent work, he recommended that I check out a band called "Sleeper" whom I'd never heard of before. I ended up following this lead and hitched around 200 miles to watch the band perform at a venue called the Barrowlands in Glasgow, Scotland. I was traveling on a budget of twelve and a half pounds a day, so spending ten pounds on a small band was quite a commitment and the change to my schedule required me to spend an extra night sleeping in the countryside outside of Glasgow. As it turned out, I slept next to a lake and woke up to one of the most beautiful sunrises I've ever seen. These experiences, caused by the difficulties of attending the concert, added immeasurably to my enjoyment of it. I was there for the support acts (who were great, incidentally) and was eventually pushed up against the front as the Glaswegians piled in, got drunk, and then proceeded to jump around me, singing bawdy chants between songs. The performance was fantastic, the audience was a significant part of the experience, and I made a few friends. Once the performance was over I realized my watch had come off in the "fray," and while searching for it in the debris at the front of the stage, I managed to find about 20 pounds in dropped money. I also found my watch. I had never heard of Sleeper before and neither had anybody I knew; nevertheless, as I walked back to my hostel I felt I'd been somehow blessed to come across them and experience them in that moment, not to mention the tidy profit I'd made during the night. Every part of the experience was in some sense itinerant—a product of a random event which inspired a series of other random events, all of which conspired to produce a sense of jouissance.

Considering these various experiences, it is difficult for me to accept that many of them can be authentically reproduced using digital technology, as it currently exists. I am a huge fan of attempts to capture the live experience and make that more accessible, but I fear that to move all live music to the digital realm would undermine an important aspect of culture. While we should seek to make live events more accessible through digital means, we should not deprioritize the physical accessibility of live music for all.

As someone who still performs in front of crowds for a job (albeit as a lecturer) I also feel that the aura of the audience is as important as the aura of the artist or the art. When one can see, or indeed feel, the responsiveness of an audience, it stimulates inspiration, commitment, and dedication; moreover, it gives the performer an opportunity to express their full identity. Hence the folk tales of musicians driven to do secret gigs while recording, to remind them why they make music in the first place. As Arendt identifies, we can express ourselves in any number of forums but the more visceral, plural, and responsive the forum, the more we come to know who we actually are (Kristeva, 2001, p. 174). The benefits for the artist of live, physical events, in terms of their iterative and interactive opportunities, cannot be easily replicated online. For this reason, as long as we still have musical artists I expect that we will still have live events.

For the audience, the possibility of unanticipated public action is such an important part of live music that digital attempts to replicate the experience should do their best to replicate the haphazard nature of "real" live events; whether that be through facilitating introductions to others in the crowd, through allowing the viewer to exercise agency over their vantage point, or through demanding a certain amount of "cult activity" before access is granted. These elements could add to the aura which surrounds a live music event and thus contribute to the possibility of audience members experiencing that sense of jouissance, which live music so often provides.

References

Adorno, T. & Horkheimer, M. (1997). *The dialectics of enlightenment*. London: Verso.

Arendt, H. (1958). *The human condition*. Chicago: University of Chicago Press.

Arendt, H. (1967). *The origins of totalitarianism*. London: George Allen & Unwin Ltd.

Barthes, R. (1975). *The pleasure of the text*. New York: Hill and Wang.

Benjamin, W. (1936/1968). The work of art in the age of mechanical reproduction (H. Zohn, Trans.). In Arendt, H. (Ed.), *Illuminations: essays and reflections* (pp. 1–15). New York: Schocken Books.

Cixous, H. & Clement, C. (1975). *The newly born woman* (B. Wing, Trans.) Minneapolis: University of Minnesota Press.

Deleuze, G. (2001). Dualism, monism and multiplicities. *Contretemps*, 2, 92–108.

Deleuze, G. & Guattari, F. (1987). *A thousand plateaus: Capitalism and schizophrenia* (B. Massumi, Trans.). Minneapolis: University of Minnesota Press.

Jenkins, H. (2006). *Convergence culture: Where old and new media collide*. New York: New York University Press.

Kristeva, J. (2001). *Hannah Arendt* (R. Guberman, Trans.). New York: Columbia University Press.

Lacan, J. (1992). *The seminar, Book VII: The ethics of psychoanalysis*. New York: Norton.

Marx, K. (1973). *Grundrisse* (M. Nicolaus, Trans.) New York: Vintage.

Merchart, O. (2006). Time for a new beginning. Arendt, Benjamin and the messianic conception of political temporality. *Rediscriptions*, 10, 134–149.

Poster, M. (1997). Cyberdemocracy: The Internet and the public sphere. In D. Holmes (Ed.), *Virtual politics: Identity and community in cyberspace* (pp. 212–228). London: Sage.

Van Buskirk, E. (2009). *4 ways live and digital music are teaming up to rock your world*. Retrieved from http://www.wired.com/2009/11/4-ways-live-and-digital-music-are-teaming-up-to-rock-your-world.

Yauch, A. (2006). *Awesome; I Fuckin' Shot That!*. London: Oscilloscope Laboratories.

What's my scene: festival fandom and the applification of the Big Day Out stage

3

A. Jones

What's my scene still tryin' to find my scene
What's my scene still tryin' to find my scene

Seth Sentry (2012)

3.1 Introduction

Seth Sentry's "My Scene" narrates the artist's journey through a number of ill-fitting subcultures in search of a "scene." Ending with the words "it's the hardest thing to do, to look like them but feel like you" concludes one "weirdo's" (Sentry, 2012) musical lament of not fitting in, and questioning whether he needs to. However, irony infuses the bars of this "Aussie" hit. The lyrics are effortlessly delivered with the Australian twang and underscored with a lazy backbeat that places this track, and Sentry, in the growing genre of Australian hip-hop. Yet artists like Sentry are often seen sharing the stages of the festival circuit with musicians from an array of scenes, rather than the genre (or complementary genres) specific festivals of the 1980s and 1990s.

A scene in the context of this discussion refers to a music scene, which is the expression of a shared identity through music, aesthetics and performance (Bennett and Peterson, 2004, p. 2). While a scene might comprise only one genre of music, a scene is more than just music. While "scene" music festivals still exist, the 2000s represented the era of the multiscene music festivals. The multiscene festival is not new—Woodstock is an example of such an event—however, this chapter argues that the range of genres at a single festival has expanded and the reason for attending these festivals has changed. From counter-cultural rebellion to the celebration of the self, this chapter discusses the history of the Big Day Out (BDO) and its fan-base. It looks at the past, present, and future of live music festivals, and examines how technological changes in music consumption are not congruous with an equal style of consuming live music events.

While it was predicted that the digital evolution of recorded music would see the demise of live music consumption, it has been recognized that the opposite has actually happened—as we discover more ways to consume music digitally, music consumers seem to be craving music in the live form. One bastion of live music consumption has been the music festival, a communal celebration of music, aesthetics, and style. Music festivals in the early 2000s saw a growth in number and participation.

The Digital Evolution of Live Music

One type of festival that became particularly dominant during this time in Australia was the touring, single-day music festival. This chapter explores the similarities and connections between the rise in digital consumption practices and the rise (and fall) of the single-day multiscene festival.

While this chapter considers a number of festivals, it will use Australia's longest running single-day touring festival, the BDO, as its focus. Considering the BDO's transformation from independent to multiscene festival, while remaining only one day long, and the challenges that it faced, this chapter reflects on the rise and fall of the BDO line-up, which led to its cancelation in 2014. It ponders the loss in fan identification with the festival and loss of festival identity. The central premise behind this chapter is that the single-day multiscene festival has come to resemble a digital music application and fans do not want to consume "live" music in this way. Such a discussion requires understanding music festival history, associated (changing) fandoms, as well as technological developments in music consumption that were happening throughout these times.

3.2 A brief history of music festivals: 1960s–1990s

> It was 1996 and I stood in cut-off army pants and a Punky Brewster t-shirt on an oval in Fremantle watching Beck and the Beastie Boys in a beat box battle from one stage to another. On the same day, my drummer, Alex, got Dave Grohl's autograph for me and I picked up Rancid's guitar strings. I was crushed in the Foo Fighter's moshpit, but it was worth it because I got to see Dave Grohl close up on stage. It was my first music festival. I remember the sweat. I remember the heat. I remember the bands ... but most of all I remember the fans. People like me: grunge, indie, skater kids together celebrating our love of our scene.

Music festivals have a long history of social resistance (Abrahams, 1982; Sharpe, 2008; Turner, 1982; Waterman, 1998). Sharp and others note that festivals provide a way for groups to gain control over cultural space, challenge dominant ideologies, and move specific issues to the center. This happens particularly when an event is organized around a culture or identity that is marginalized in dominant culture (Sharpe, 2008, 218; Jackson, 1992; Kates & Belk, 2001). Woodstock, Monterey, the Isle of Wight, and the Altamont festival in the 1960s are often cited as the start of the counter-cultural music festival. In the era of the rock music festival, Woodstock is recognized as the iconic counter-cultural festival in the Summer of Love. This era saw the birth of youth culture, which was fuelled by rock rebellion, a sexual revolution, and antiwar politics. Kitts writes that "more than anything else, the sonics of rock music literalized the breaking, expanding, or blurring of boundaries" (2009, p. 717). Music festival fans were becoming children of the revolution, not a mirror of their parents. The Isle of Wight, Glastonbury, and the US festivals all carried undertones of political activism, social rebellion, and a festival of the "we." While it has been suggested that the presence of bikies at Altamont in 1969 killed the vibe and was the end of "counter-culture" festival as it had been known (Kitts, 2009), the large-scale festivals infused with the concepts of "freedom" and "humanitarianism" continued through the 1970s and 1980.

The 1990s saw a change in the festival scene when annual music festivals were embedded into fans' calendars across the United Kingdom, United States, and Australia. These festivals contained headlining acts situated in the genres and subgenres of rock, indie, grunge, and punk. The popularity of grunge/alternative "indie" music (born out of the punk rock scene in the 1980s) saw rock music festivals such as Lollapalooza, Coachella, and the BDO become embedded in the musical calendar, but also move from one-offs to festivals that toured around countries and, some the world.

From 2000 to 2010 there was what can only be described as an explosion of festivals on the summer festival circuit across the United States, United Kingdom, and Australia. The early 2000s saw an increase in the traveling festival and the arrival of the Electronic Dance Music (EDM) festival for fans of genres and subgenres of electronic dance music: Godskitchen, Stereosonic, Cream/Creamfields, Vibes on a Summer's Day, and more were added to the summer festival circuit; rap/hip-hop festivals followed suit, and soon there was a genre festival catering to almost every music scene.

Fans of a scene are in search of a tangible fan experience at a festival. They perform their fandom, within the context of a musical scene that is shaped by a set of unwritten rules for participation. Participants in scenes share an appreciation of music, aesthetics, values, and politics, which while often a lifestyle was no more apparent than the fandom displayed at the music festivals aligned with their scene(s) or subculture(s). Bennett and Peterson note the importance of differentiating between scene and subculture because subculture "presumes that society has one commonly shared culture from which subculture is deviant" (2004, p. 3). Shank argues that scenes are a necessary part of generating "exciting" and new forms of music (Shank, 1994, p. 122) and music festivals, as transnational mega-events, play an intrinsic role in forging and maintaining music scenes. Music festivals provide a space for learning, engaging with, and performing the cultural practices of a scene through a complex array of semiotic activities such as dancing, listening, talking, and, since the popularity of hand-held smartphone technology, recording and uploading. Straw notes that there is a constant negotiation within scenes regarding the relationship between "speech and noise, noise and music, attention and distraction, human movement and the physical forms that enclose it" (Straw, 2001, p. 247). Each scene is its own culture, with its own rules for engagement. Fans of a scene understand how to engage authentically at a live event.

If audience movement is considered, it will show how various scenes express themselves through complex semiotic codes. Shank argues that "a scene itself can be defined as an over productive signifying community" (1994, p. 122) and at a multigenre festival, members of particular scenes communicate their preferred musical genres through their dress and actions. Heavy rock audiences perform the "wall of death," where two walls of fans face each other and then run toward each other periodically throughout the set. Within hip-hop scenes, there is the bounce, with "wave your hands in the air" gesticulation, or popping and locking for the hardcore dancers. EDM often includes the dance circle, made up of traditional candy ravers, drum-bass-running-mans, big-beat groovers, breakbeat twisters, and the "old school" "peg-the-washing" dance. In new-folk town, bearded hipsters stand and sway, or sit on the lawn, while they instagram beanie selfies. While some ways of engaging with fandom might be subtler than a wall of death, all of the previous scenes are physical and tangible, and fans engage with music, while participating and supporting their scene.

3.3 The 1990s to the 2000s

I have many memories of the Big Day Out, as a devotee from 1996 to the early 2000s. Among the moshpit memories are the ones where I was in danger of getting crushed while bouncing up and down to bands such as Soundgarden, Korn, and Jebediah. One particular, I remember when Hole's bouncer pulled me over the barrier and Courtney Love pulled me up on stage and I was saved from further crushing. My favorite memory at the BDO was in 2000 when my brother, my friend, and I dressed up as the Beastie Boys. They weren't playing, but Beastie Boys were a band that was part of the scene at the festival. We spent the day dancing with other Beastie fans to other bands. We made new friends through this performance of fandom, and every time I see a yellow hard hat, it takes me back to that day. The moments, as fans, that we take from these events not only transcend the wire fences of the venue, but add to the identity of the event itself.

The BDO was Australia's longest-running traveling music festival with a transgressive evolution. The single day event evolved from an independent rock festival into a multiscene festival. Music pioneers, Ken West and Vivian Lees, began the BDO in 1992, and they are now infamous for bringing Nirvana to the Australian stage at the time when the grunge icons moshed their way to global fame. It started as a day-long festival in Sydney and commenced touring to Adelaide, Melbourne, and Perth in 1993. The initial line-up of bands included those from complimentary indie-rock "scenes." At the time, West had a clear vision for the BDO:

> *Rock festivals—at least in Australia—before the Big Day Out were all about pretending to be Woodstock... in the countryside, drinking beer and getting stoned. Normally it was a camp-out and facilities were shit, the production was shit and if it rained it was a mudfest. I hated that whole hippy bullshit concept. I hated hippies full stop. I wanted urban mayhem, I wanted controlled chaos, but I also wanted cold drinks, nice food, lots of choice, good drainage, lots of toilets and great production. Then I wanted people to learn about music, go as hard as they wanted and be able to get home safely at the end of the night.*
>
> *Howarth (2006) and Langlands (2012)*

The BDO brought together large independent rock acts, which were complemented with local Australian artists. The first BDO had 21 bands and ticket prices were $40. The festival became a pilgrimage for fans, who donned their "festival attire"—namely a band t-shirt, some cut-off army pants, a pair of Chucks/Doc Martens, colored hair, and DIY attitudes—and joined fellow lovers of rock music to show allegiance to their favorite bands and perform their fandom.

The BDO dominated the festival circuit in the 1990s and was one of the only festivals that gave indie kids the time and space to perform their local fandom to global artists. The 1990s represents an era "when fans were marginal to the operations of our culture, ridiculed in the media, shrouded in the underground" (Jenkins, 2006, p. 1). Youth culture (the dominant attendees of events) was dangerous and the music was tinny, loud and contained too much reverb. "Indie"—independent (UK and Australia)—or alternative (USA) rock glistened with anti-establishment spikes of 1970s and 1980s punk, where the anti-pop music and labels who recorded them made significant inroads challenging the major record labels (Hesmondhalgh, 1999, p. 35). With digital technology only just emerging, music festivals offered a local space to commune with like-minded fans of local and international bands and celebrate fandom. The mid-to-late 1990s began to see music festivals labeled, marketed, and consumed. The V Festival (Virgin Media sponsored) is an example of this, as is the Vans Warped Tour. By the end of the 1990s, the counter-cultural elements that still underpinned the DIY ethos of the music festival as an alternative celebration had been usurped by the idea that one could buy an identity with an entry ticket.

3.4 The 2000s: the applification of the BDO stage

I remember it was 1996 and I was in my house in Kardinya Western Australia. I was sitting in my room, my canary yellow walls were covered in Nirvana posters and I was listening to Triple J, waiting by my tape deck to record "Big Me" by the Foo Fighters. I can't remember where I was when I downloaded Macklemore and Ryan Lewis' "Thrift Shop" on my iPhone last year. We are now constantly "integrating music into our personal spaces" (Wilson, 2013). But I worry that now with such ease of access, fans are losing their connection to physical time and space, and tangible fan moments.

By 2010 the festival line-ups in Australia, including the BDO, were akin to a YouTube mash-up, where pop, rock, punk, hip-hop, EDM, electro, dub-step, D&B, and R&B could all be found on a festival bill. For the BDO, there was no longer an underlying counter-cultural thread that wove acts together. Not only had the individual genres been fused together but also mainstream genres were now a part of the mix—Kanye West and Soundgarden on the 2012 BDO line-up, for instance. While the genre-specific festival did not die out completely, many went underground, many reduced in size, and others simply morphed into multiscene festivals. Godskitchen, a strictly dance music festival, was rebranded to Global Gathering, a festival that moved from dance-music genres to include dance, rock, and hip-hop. Rising in popularity from in 2006 to a crash in 2014, the single-day multiscene festival has dominated the Australian music festival circuit.

Underscoring this change in festival line-ups was a change in technology, and the types of technology used to consume music. If the 1990s was the era of the (mix) tape, the Walkman, compact disc, the Discman, and CD stackers, then 2000–2010 was the era of .wav files, file-sharing, MP3s, MP4s, and MP3 players. Then 2010 until 2013 has been the era of smartphones, docking stations, Bluetooth, high-quality headphones, and an abundance of applications for listening to, sharing, and downloading music. Fans have gone from their "local" position in the 1990s—listening for a song at home, on the radio to be played, with their fingers pressed on the record and play button on a tape deck so they can record it—to the "global" in 2013—where applications such as Spotify and RDio allow fans to be their own radio DJs. Fans no longer have to sit and wait for a tape deck, or even a computer, to play, because an application on their smartphone can play what they want instantly. Wilson writes:

> *Over the past hundred years of recorded music, people have progressively integrated music into their personal space. Music is given meaning by the way it was consumed. From the gramophone to the iPod playlist, a notion of time and place has been integral to the listen activity.*
>
> *Wilson (2013)*

The relationship to "time" and fandom has changed through the applification of music. Bull suggests that the consumer of music through digital devices such as the iPod "struggles to achieve a level of autonomy over time and place through the creation of a privatized auditory bubble" (Bull, 2005, p. 303). Smartphones and streaming devices allow a listener to soundtrack their lives, but placing this "auditory bubble" around them also creates a sensory division between time and space.

Applications have changed how people procure and consume music. Now, there is no need to wait for an obscure song to come on the radio, nor do fans have to buy a whole album just for a secret song on the b-side. With streaming, listeners do not even have to download a song, or know that it exists, because our software will find it, describe it, and play it. For example the "Genius" function in iTunes automatically produces playlists as well as suggestion for future purchases based on its ongoing compilation and analysis of the users' pattern of purchasing and listening choices. There is no serendipity or surprise in such algorithmic suggestions (Wilson, 2013, p. 118). Digital music applications, with their array of music choices, encourage the listener to "become the average of his or her own listening tastes" (Wilson, 2013), becoming a fan of everything and yet a fan of nothing. Applications and ease of access to musical abundance allow musical consumers the ability to soundtrack their lives.

This abundance of choice denies the time to be fans. The ease of access means that listeners no longer have to put the time in to be fans. Time spent trawling through CD racks for the b-side on that rare album, or traveling to New York to see an underground band play in a basement, are tangible experiences that make time and space for fandom. Access to such songs and events, however, are now available with through an "app" and Google. The fact that musical consumers can now access a musical experience so easily then lessens its cultural significance. The buzz of the "find" of discovering that "rare" piece of musical history lessens, as everything is readily available in the "cloud." One result of fans no longer needing to dedicate the "time" to their musical consumption is musical nomadism, the movement from the "we"—physically identifying with a scene—to the I—digitally sampling, programming, and soundtracking one's life with the abundance of music available. This digital consumption of music has had an impact on the relationship between music, fandom, and scene identification at music festivals. The "experience economy" (Pine & Gilmore, 2007) on which music festivals are based became increasingly important, as tangible, physical, scene experiences became a rarity for fans. Arguably then, digital technology has actually strengthened ties between scene members as they seek to retain the space of the music festival space to perform their allegiance to the scene. The BDO originally offered the time and space for fans to perform such affiliations, and this in turn built and sustained its global identity as one of the best one-day rock festivals in the 1990s (Shinnen, 2014). However, following in the footsteps of digital counterparts, the physical line-up before its cancelation in 2014 was suffering from a case of musical nomadism.

The final Big Day Out I attended was in 2011, and it was the last probably because I just wasn't feeling 'it' anymore. This might have had something to do with the fact that I was now in my mid 20s but I honestly felt it was more than this. It just didn't feel like the BDO anymore. I spent so much time walking from one stage to another and barely getting to see any of the bands I had gone there to see. I felt I had paid over $165 to walk around getting annoyed at all the festival fans who just seemed to be there to get drunk and naked. For me the festival existed physically, but was over for me emotionally.

Music festivals, however, are an experience, not disassociated musical bits and bytes that have been digitally mastered. They are beer, sweat, sun, costumes, merchandise, loud music, and the fans that make it live and breathe, something that fans can view through a screen cannot touch, feel, and live unless they are present at the venue. Digital technology has changed how we consume "live music," in terms of what we constitute as live (Bennett, 2012), and this has highlighted the relationship between artist and album, album and single. The breakdown of a whole album to a number of disassociated songs consequently challenges the concept or need for an album to be created at all, and applications such as Spotify, RDio and even the older iTunes genius playlists encourage this musical nomadism. With digital consumption, practices becoming more and more fragmented, and it appears that the need for an artist to have any more than one good song is diminishing.

As Hall suggests, *how* music is consumed "can be discursively re-articulated to construct new meanings, connect with different social practices, and position social subjects differently" (Hall, 1988, p. 9). This is recognized with the emergences of the music festival fan. The music festival fan is a fan of the music festival experience, and is the equivalent of a walking mixtape. Their allegiance is not limited to one particular music festival. They are there for the music festival experience, rather than to engage with a particular music scene. The festival fans are musical nomads that are not bound by the same rules, connections, and subcultural/scene affiliations as their fixed fan counterparts. In fact their permutations are limitless, which allows their movement through, and dominance within, multiple festival spaces. Festival fans represent a postmodern fan conception that is characterized by multiplicities, so interactions and movements between multiple songs and scenes occur, rather than a "sedentary" (Gedalof, 2000, pp. 341–342) musical affiliation with a specific genre, album, or artist.

The postmodern festival fan straddles musical boundaries and enjoys an individually customized and random experience of *music*. Consequentially the music festival fan or musical nomad has a different relationship to the festival space to that of fans of the scene. Lundy (2013) suggests that the nomad "is largely predicated on their differing relations to space, and more precisely, their distribution *of* and *in* space" (p. 234). When approaching the festival fans as musical nomads, the primary focus is on not their capacity to move beyond a single festival space, but their ability to resist fixed identification with a particular scene. However, as recognized with the demise of the BDO, the festival fan is not enough to sustain a multiscene one-day festival.

What made the BDO work were the links to the links to the indie music scene and the performance, as well as the embodiment of this fandom in a communal space. While technology is great for individual customisation of musical playlists, a festival needs that thread of community and like-mindedness to maintain its identity. Without it the scene is void of meaning and authenticity. What the demise of the multimusic scene shows us is that fans want those physical tangible moments with the bands. For fans of the scenes, live music remains one of those occasions for a tangible "rare" find or a buzz that belongs to us. A music festival cannot resemble an iTunes playlist, it is not the Internet, it is a live music experience, and fans want to keep it that way. This is recognized with the demise of the BDO festival.

Year by year, the BDO festival expanded its line-up and as it did it weakened its identity. It became more and more expensive to tour the country with the expanding line-ups, riders, and crews. Shinnen wrote that since 2011, "the festival's reputation as a cutting edge and guaranteed sellout success has waned" (2014), attendance declined in 2013, even with big-named acts still on the line-up. It seems that the BDO reputation was marred with Blur pulling out of the line-up, as well as the increase in ticket price to AU$185. Fans of the scene(s) who attended the festival felt ripped off, and festival fans complained about poor facilities and "expensive beer." Famed musical promoter A.J. Maddah (whose successful festivals include Soundwave, Warped and the recently canceled Harvest festivals) became co-owner of the BDO in 2013, along with US company C3, to try to save the ailing music festival.

In an interview with alternative radio station Triple J, Maddah addressed some of the challenges with the BDO. He acknowledged: "BDO is more about the experience. It's more about the day. You know there are 3 or 4 bands everyone wants to see throughout the programming hopefully .... And for that—$185 is absolutely unreasonable" (Tilley, 2014). There were over 100 bands on the lineup for the festival that year. It was not just the price of the tickets. The line-up resembled a Spotify playlist more than ever. It had become both too expensive and too eclectic. There just was not enough time in a single day for fans to enjoy their favorite bands. As one contributor to the Triple J interview commented, "the reason the BDO has turned so crap recently is because it has no identity. Look at the festivals that are killing it: Splendor, Falls, Laneway, and even Stereo. They know who they want to target" (Tilley, 2014). The festival made the fatal mistake of forgetting what it was and that fans had a connection with this former identity. To this, Maddah's interview response was:

> *The Big Day Out always has a tough task because it tries to bring so many tribes together, rather than be a dance festival or be a metal festival. So that's always going to be tough. But you do it by making sure your ticket is reasonably priced and that all of those groups you're trying to get in, they need to get value. If a ticket's $160, the dance crowd needs to feel like they've got $200 value, the rock crowd needs to feel that they've got $200 value, the indie people think they've got that much value. So it's about coherent programming and making sure that all of the people that you've brought together feel like they've got good value for their ticket.*
>
> *Tilley (2014)*

While it seems that Maddah acknowledges the need to feel that each scene has gained "value" with their entry, he does not demonstrate an awareness that maybe too many scenes were being brought together or that possibly the BDO has strayed too far from its independent roots. This interview took place in February 2014, and on June 26, 2014, it was made public that US company C3 (owners of Lollapalooza) had taken ownership of BDO and it had been canceled for 2015. What ensued was a mix of responses from fans, music journalists, and enthusiasts, but one point that most agreed on was that "it must be acknowledged that in its heyday the BDO was one of the premier rock'n'roll shows of its kind anywhere in the world" (Shinnen, 2014).

The rise and subsequent fall of the BDO came via its loss in identity and subsequent loss in the trust of its fans. The local fans gave the BDO its indie credibility, and this was built into its framework and success as one of the world's best rock'n'roll festivals. In its shift from representing the indie scene, presenting cutting-edge acts on a stage, to a staged mass Internet-like experience, the air of counter-culture and something unique was lost, and the BDO began to die. In its heyday BDO was not a "brand," and it was a day of subcultural fandom, counter-culture expression, a DIY ethos, and a lot of rock'n'roll. In the end, it resembled a cacophony where any act from Soundgarden to Kanye could be found on contemporary line-ups. The festival lacked the subcultural thread or the thread of scenes that tied these together.

It should be noted that the mash-up of scenes at a multigenre festival works well for fans when there is time and space for punters to connect with their preferred scene or move between scenes. Festivals such as Glastonbury, Leeds, and Splendor in the Grass, which span multiple days, are prime examples of the longevity of multiscene festivals that do this well. They allow space and time for multiple scenes to co-exist in the festival space. Extra time allows multiple "scenes" to join the line-up without watering down the individual fan experience. However, when there is not enough time and space to provide festival-goers with tangible moments of fan engagement, fans become disenfranchised, and the result is that the festival loses its attraction as a fully immersive scene experience. If festivals like the BDO want to provide patrons with a "fast" or abundant musical experience, they must allow the time and space for it to happen in the parameters of the festival's "slow" form.

This is one of the failings of the single-day multiscene music festival. Due to the expanse in line-ups, and the spread of scenes, it does not allow the time and space for fans of a band or scene to adequately perform their fandom and have authentic fan moments. Contemporary multiscene single day music festival line-ups, such as the BDO like our (insert mobile device) playlists, became a mash-up of disparate genres/ scenes that have been pushed onto competing stages, and dictated to play within a particular time frame—approximately 10 hours The hyper-personalization of music that digital music applications promote has flowed on to the hyper-personalization of the multiscene music festivals, and the emergence of the 'festival fan', who, like their iTunes list, are seeking a disparate collection of musical moments, and a more fluid fandom, which is based on constantly deleting, capturing, and replacing their musical affiliations. If we extend this musical analogy, the future of mixtape or iTunes list fandom, like the technology that recorded it, is likely to be relegated to the "dustbin of history" (Marcus, 1995). "How" and "what" people consume through digital technology has reshaped "what" is being programmed for stages at music festivals like the BDO. However, the "how" fans want to consume music at one-day music festivals has not changed, in that there is still only one day to "fit in" the expanding playlist of bands. This "playlist" style of festival makes the assumption that audiences and fans wish to consume their live music in the same way as their digital practices. The demise of festivals such as the BDO suggests otherwise. With the cancelation of the BDO in 2014, the swing toward the digital playlist style of programming was not working for fans and promoters alike. This is recognized through the popularity of niche festivals, where authentic fan moments can be collected.

3.5 The future of music festivals

> When my inbox pings with an email advertising the latest music festival, I always open it and peruse the playlist. Pushing feelings of ageing aside—I am still up (or is it down?) with contemporary indie music—I pondered as to why I still must check the "line-up." It is because I am searching for that "line-up" that excited me the way that of the Big Day Out did. Even as I head toward my mid-30s I still want a place to perform my fandom. I don't see this as an age thing, I see it as a fan thing.

Today the future success of single-day events needs to look backward to the niche-focused festivals: smaller or genre-specific events. The success of Soundwave (genre) and the more contemporary Laneway (limited sales and complementary genres) festivals demonstrates, as A.J. Maddah might say, what "the punters want." Darren Levin, Editor-in-chief for Faster and Louder, one of Australia's premier music websites, says that at a music event, the younger audience "want craft beer, they want a bit more of an experience, not just to be put in a big, huge racecourse and sold a few dagwood dogs" (Law, 2014). Fans do not want fewer music festivals, just fewer bands at them, as they are in search of an authentic fan experience. Pine and Gilmore (1999) suggest that "authenticity" is the "primary source of differentiation" when dealing with economies of experience and if the music festival does not have a clear identity, fans feel as if it is a "staged experience," and it leaves them "longing for less contrived encounters" (Pine & Gilmore, 2007, p. 12).

Boutique festivals such as *Listen Out* with its tagline "the best, not the biggest", with limited acts and limited tickets, embody the future of music festival experiences. In contemporary Australian culture, the desire for what can be seen as tangible and unique activities extends beyond music festivals.

In popular culture and beyond, there has been a cultural swing toward the need to engage and create "meaningful" experiences, such as "authentic education," "raw food," and the fascination with the regrowth of the hipster. The desire and ability to access more of the world digitally is seemingly being co-balanced with a desire for live, physical, real, and unique experiences. What was demonstrated in the demise of the BDO was not a dislike of a music festival per se, but a collective denouncement of this model of "Internet on a stage" style of programming. The sustainment of the genre-specific and niche events proves that consumers still highly value the live music event. However, the cancelation of the BDO shows that traditional music festival modes of programming, which include limiting the number of bands and genres on a stage in one day, have survived the test of time. Just because fans of music want the freedom to be able to access music digitally does not mean that they want to consume all musical experiences this way. To make a music festival successful, there is a need to maintain a core identity. This will be achieved if the festival resonates with fans and allows time and space for fans of the scene or festival to engage in the experience. Keep the circle of death away from the hipsters and everything will be OK.

References

Abrahams, R. D. (1982). The language of festivals: Celebrating the economy. In V. Turner (Ed.), *Celebration: Studies in festivity and ritual* (pp. 161–177). Washington, DC: Smithsonian Institution Press.

Bennett, L. (2012). Patterns of listening through social media: Online fan engagement with the live music experience. *Social Semiotics*, 22(5), 545–557.

Bennett, A. & Peterson, R. (2004). Introduction. In A. Bennett & R. A. Peterson (Eds.), *Music Scenes: Local, Trans-Local and Virtual*. Nashville: University of Vanderbilt Press.

Bull, M. (2005). No dead Aie! The iPod and the culture of mobile listening. *Leisure Studies*, 24(4), 343–355.

Gedalof, I. (2000). Identity in transit: Nomads, cyborgs, and women. *European Journal of Women's Studies*, 7, 337–354.

Hall, S. (1988). *The hard road to renewal: Thatcherism and the crisis of the left*. London: Verso Books.

Hesmondhalgh, D. (1999). Indie: The institutional politics and aesthetics of a popular music genre. *Cultural Studies*, 13(1), 34–61.

Howarth, S. (2006). *Peace love and brown rice: A photographic history of the Big Day Out*. Brunswick: Sophie Howarth Photography.

Jackson, P. (1992). The politics of the streets: A geography of Caribana. *Political Geography*, 11, 130–151.

Jenkins, H. (2006). *Fans, bloggers, and gamers*. New York and London: New York University Press.

Kates, S. M. & Belk, R. W. (2001). The meanings of lesbian and gay pride day: Resistance through consumption and resistance to consumption. *Journal of Contemporary Ethnography*, 30(4), 392–429.

Kitts, T. (2009). Documenting, creating, and interpreting moments of definition: Monterey pop, Woodstock, and gimme shelter. *The Journal of Popular Culture*, 42(4), 715–731.

Langlands, A. (2012). *Big Day Out: Best bits of years gone*. Retrieved from http://musicfeeds.com.au/news/big-day-out-best-bits-of-years-gone.

Law, J. (2014). *With the 2015 Big Day Out cancelled, it's time to put the ageing rock festival to bed for good.* Retrieved from http://www.news.com.au.

Lundy, C. (2013). Who are our nomads today?: Deleuze's political ontology and the revolutionary problematic. *Deleuze Studies*, 7(2), 231–249.

Marcus, G. (1995). *The dustbin of history*. Cambridge, MA: Harvard University Press.

Pine, B. & Gilmore, J. (1999). *The experience economy*. Boston: Harvard Business School Press.

Pine, B. J. & Gilmore, J. H. (2007). *Authenticity: What consumers really want*. Boston: Harvard Business School Press.

Sentry, S. (2012). My scene. *This was tomorrow*. Surry Hills: High Score Records/Inertia.

Shank, B. (1994). *Dissonant identities: The rock'n'roll scene in Austin, Texas*. Hanover and London: Wesleyan University Press.

Sharpe, E. (2008). Festivals and social change: Intersections of pleasure and politics at a community music festival. *Leisure Sciences: An Interdisciplinary Approach*, 30(3), 217–234.

Shinnen, I. (2014). *Big Day Out 2015 cancelled, ending institution that introduced Nirvana*. Retrieved from http://www.theaustralian.com.au.

Straw, W. (2001). Scenes and sensibilities. *Public*, 22/23, 245–257.

Tilley, T. (2014). Big Day Out: *AJ Maddah talks to Hack*. Retrieved from http://www.abc.net.au/triplej/hack/stories/s4034027.htm.

Turner, V. W. (1982). *From ritual to theater: The human seriousness of play*. New York: Performing Arts Journal Publications.

Waterman, S. (1998). Carnivals for elites? The cultural politics of arts festivals. *Progress in Human Geography*, 22(1), 54–74.

Wilson, J. (2013). *Spotify is ruining the way we listen to classical music*. Retrieved from http://blogs.telegraph.co.uk/technology/jeremywilson2.

Section Two

Digital live

Live sound and the disappearing digital

4

J. Mulder

4.1 Introduction

In this chapter I offer a detailed production-level perspective on the advent of the digital era, specifically at the use of electronic amplification at popular music concerts. This micro-perspective can be contrasted by developments on the scale of global music industry macroeconomics. The impact of the master of all digital technologies—the Internet—on traditional monetizing options has supported a growth in live music revenue in comparison to recorded music (Holt, 2010; Mortimer, Nosko, & Sorensen, 2012; Rogers, 2013).[1] That growth has accelerated the globalization of booking agencies, ticketing companies, and venue management into a few monopolists such as Live Nation after its merger with Ticketmaster (Rogers, 2013, p. 119). These developments in turn have increased the demands on the many live sound technology providers and triggered a new level of professionalization.

Focusing on the use of digital technology at a live sound production level, I argue that although digital tools are now ubiquitous, the impact of those tools on pop music performance is not as dramatic. However, two developments do stand out: firstly with the stabilization of digital tools in live sound production, the notion that a pop concert is a replication of a studio recording has become even more apparent. Most digital processes in use replicate the tools that were available in the analog era and standard equipment in the recording studio. Interestingly, the digital versus analog debate that still rages in the professional studio, home recording, and consumer markets have lost ground in this context, in favor of the digital technology. The add-ons or plug-ins available for Digital Audio Workstations (DAWs) are minutely reverse engineered software copies of popular analog devices. The graphic interfaces of such plug-ins are made to look exactly like the older, often vintage, hardware equivalents.

Secondly, increasing computational power has allowed for pitch processing to be real-time, either to create artistic effects, for example, the "Cher" or "gerbil effect" (Frere-Jones, 2008), or to correct vocal pitch to a technical optimum. Such processing was impossible to achieve with predigital technologies, but now a singer's voice can be corrected when it is out of tune with great ease and in real-time. This adds an intriguing level of complexity debates around what constitutes a "live" performance, including terms of fairness, or accusations of cheating. Such terms are comparable to a long history of lip-syncing "incidents," as reported for instance by Steve Wurtzler

[1] The bulk of these revenues are, however, created by a small number of older, long-established acts such as Bruce Springsteen, Madonna, and Bon Jovi.

The Digital Evolution of Live Music

(1992) and Philip Auslander (2008). Pretend-performance issues appear to be endemic to Superbowl shows, but there are other examples. Renowned classical cellist Yo-Yo Ma performed a work by contemporary American composer John Adams at Barack Obama's inauguration, accompanied by a few fellow classical stars (Wakin, 2009). For a number of reasons (including the freezing outdoor temperatures) the performers pretended to play along to a recording of a rehearsal some days earlier.

In 2007, Billy Joel was incorrectly accused of lip-syncing when playing and singing the anthem at the Superbowl. In clips of the television broadcast the brief effect of a pitch corrector becoming activated can be heard, causing some accusations of cheating on social and traditional media. According to his own account his foldback monitors were not working so he did not receive adequate feedback of his singing and the accuracy of his pitch in relation to the piano he was playing.[2] The first few notes he sang were slightly out of tune, causing an eager TV broadcast engineer to activate (or "insert") the digital pitch correction. It is likely that the corrected voice would have been audible to the broadcast audience only, as the stadium audience would have heard a different mix controlled by a live sound engineer.

This chapter concentrates on popular music performance practices as opposed to academic and avant-garde live electronic music (see for instance Emmerson, 2007). The latter embraced the digital conceptually as a site for exploration and experimentation rather than as a tool for replicating the analog. This constitutes a distinctly different practice tradition, which we can consider as being external to popular music and the discussions in this chapter. To be more specific, this chapter tends to music practices that require predominantly traditional pop and rock instruments using microphones or other transduction processes (e.g. electric guitars) in contrast to performances of DJs or other digital electronic music sources using mainly pre-produced material.

4.2 Sound is analog

Before beginning this exploratory section, it is important to underline a crucial aspect of the physics of sound. No matter the ubiquity of the digital, in name or in actual technology, sound is analog. Where mediatized sound is being produced or reproduced, a transduction process is required, through a microphone on the input side or through a loudspeaker at the output. A loudspeaker transduces electronic waveforms into audible sound waves. Sound data that is kept or processed in the digital domain needs to be converted from the digital to the electronic before it can be transduced to audible sound. On the other end of the chain, whether for recording, broadcast, telephony, or amplification, where a sound source (voice, musical instrument, a barking dog, etc.) is being picked up, the reverse process is required. In the case of electronic sound amplification or reinforcement (further to be referred to as "live sound"), some digital processing may take place in between the transduction and conversion stages, but input (microphones, electric guitars etcetera) and output are ultimately analog.

[2] Billy Joel shared his experience of that night on the Howard Stern Radio Show on October 20, 2010, 7:05 am.

With every generation of sound engineering technology, the analog to digital conversion process moves a little closer to the actual transduction stage of audible sound to electronic waveforms. For instance, although not commonplace, analog to digital converters can now reside inside a microphone (Becker-Foss et al., 2010). But the converter still requires an electronic waveform to digitize and the transduction process cannot be bypassed. Small improvements in technical sound quality are achieved in this way. But, microphones do still come in a range of sensitivities (to softer or louder sound) and polar diagrams (directional sensitivity), which relate to their analog working principles. Consequently, microphone selection choices have a more profound effect on the sonic outcome than any small improvements made by the advancement of digital technologies. For loudspeakers a similar development can be observed, with all-digital connections to the actual speaker cabinets, which have built-in amplifiers, potentially improving the quality of signal transfer. Even so, the basics of speaker typology, configuration, and setup continue to have a far greater impact on what an audience hears.

When comparing technical specifications, the transducers and converters are getting better over time but, as can be observed in the discussions, surrounding the digital versus analog (and the persistence of vinyl records as a consumer medium), better tools do not automatically imply better sound or a better auditory experience. Some consider the digitization process as detrimental; the fragmentation of continuous analog sound waves into separate chunks of data (samples) allegedly reduces the accuracy or even the wholeness of sound. The argumentation in these debates is fragmented and anecdotal, often focusing on, for instance, the use of (low bitrate) MP3 codecs or the inability of computers to emulate analog synthesizers convincingly.[3] Ultimately there is very little research, let alone research that uses scientifically rigorous double-blind ABX comparisons, to support claims that one or the other is the better sounding technology or practice.[4]

4.3 Digital processes in live sound

On the production level, when looking at (sound and music) the technology in use, the digital genesis spread out over four decades. Specific live sound audio signal processing has been taking place in the digital domain since the 1980s. Until the first decade of the twenty-first century, such processing took place in dedicated digital boxes (e.g. effects and system processors installed externally to a mixing desk). One of the earliest relevant tools to become digitized was the "delay line," which can be used to time-align loudspeakers (to compensate for timing differences resulting from a difference between audience and sound source and the distance between audience and loudspeaker, or between different loudspeaker systems). One of, or perhaps the first of, these digital delay tools was produced by a firm called Lexicon and designed by

[3] The issue with MP3 audio compression is documented, for instance, by Sterne (2006).

[4] A good example of how presupposed or assumed qualities of certain technologies can be debunked experimentally can be found in an elegant experiment by entertainment academic John Huntington (2011).

(among others) Barry Blesser (Blesser & Lee, 1971).[5] The need for a device that could delay sound by a few milliseconds had already been identified in 1925 (McCutchen, 1927). Before it became digitally feasible, many different tricks were tried (using hoses, tubes, and magnetic tape), but all these suffered from audible degradation in sound quality and the digital delay line proved to be a long-awaited improvement.

Digital mixing desks became available on a large scale in the 1990s but it would take up until the first decade of the 2000s for them to become mainstream; at present they are commonplace—an interesting difference with the closely related, but disparate, stage lighting discipline, which embraced digital control surfaces instantaneously when they became available in the 1980s.[6] Live sound engineers preferred to keep working on large, heavy, and expensive mixing desk that afforded immediate and hands-on access to large sets of different parameters. The large crafts often needed manual hauling into narrow positions in fixed seating theaters doing simultaneous damage to both theater furniture and technicians' backs. Producers of early digital consoles tried to reduce the footprint by offering smaller desks with fewer directly accessible parameters, with others hidden under menus and visible only on different on-screen pages.[7] That lack of immediacy and tactility is considered as one of the main reasons why it took the live sound profession such a long time to take up the digital mixing desk as their central tool. And many common digital live sound desks are still relatively large and have many dials and buttons that offer direct access to the most important parameters. In addition to a reduced footprint and weight, the ability to store some or all of the parameters and create "automation scenes" (configurations which can be instantly recalled) offered a great advantage. Currently some concert mixing is done remotely from networked tablet PCs or even smartphones, offering very few directly accessible parameters and no tactility of faders' dials and buttons at all.

4.4 Global sound design

The shift of the music industry revenue stream from the recorded to the live sped up the synchronization of amplification practices that had previously been developed and maintained locally. Major arena tours either travel with all the staging, sound, and light required or are very specific in all the elements of the sound system design. The necessary show data to drive a digital mixing desk (provided the right brand and model is available) travel on a USB stick, or remain in the cloud, saving trucking space and weight. Loudspeaker numbers, typology, and setup may still vary from venue to venue,

[5] Blesser is coauthor of a book called *Spaces Speak* (2006), which addresses the possibilities and state of the art of room acoustics and technology. Importantly, he and coauthor Linda-Ruth Salter posit that the acoustics of rooms or performance spaces are in fact technology and as such shaping the debate about the use of technology and performances of traditionally acoustic (i.e. without the use of electronic amplification) musics.

[6] An obvious development when considering the size and limitations (in terms of the ability to store cues or scenes) of predigital theatrical lighting control desks.

[7] Reducing the footprint has a strong incentive, because the mixing desk setup will take up less space, allowing more tickets to be sold.

but adaptations are made to secure a standard outcome. This praxis was common to the largest of acts such as the Rolling Stones and Madonna but has now become the norm in many international tours. A similar effect could be observed when Broadway and West End musicals became global undertakings. Not just books and scores travel, they are now accompanied by prescriptive designs—including sound designs—and often a lead sound designer, sometimes even with billing credit. The result was a uniformization of what each megamusical sounded like, with maximum consistency from night to night and venue to venue. Jonathan Burston (1998) took issue with this development, comparing megamusical sound designs to "FM sound," referring to the generalness of mass media music reproduction and broadcast. Although the analysis presented in that paper is lacking in technical accuracy, Burston's point concerning the rationalization and uniformity of live sound production is an important one.[8]

4.5 Dislocations and authenticity

In an analysis of (live) popular music, it is important to reiterate Paul Théberge's (2001, p. 3) premise with regard to popular music and technology: "...without electronic technology, popular music in the twenty-first century is unthinkable." It will come as no surprise that the bulk of this electronic technology utilizes digital processing of some form. And digital processes are facilitated by electronics (a "chip" is ultimately a large collection of very small transistors, the component that powered your radio and stereo until the 1980s); analog or digital, electrons are electrons. Ultimately all digital processing used in sound engineering and music production needs some old-fashioned electronics at some stage. Théberge raises another point that "the aesthetics of 'high-fidelity' have reinforced the idea that microphones, amplifiers and speakers are *reproductive* technologies, that they are, by design, transparent in their operation" (2001, p.3). Although any sound engineer will argue that the impact of microphone and loudspeaker choices is paramount to successful sound production, those choices apparently fail to obfuscate ideological stances with regard to digital technology. That is to say that analog transduction technology is often taken for granted while the use of digital technology is at times considered unnatural and degrading to sound, whether audible or not, for instance as argued by Jonathan Sterne (2006a). Whereas Théberge flags the issue of how technology is experienced and informs opinion, Sterne (2003, p. 285) points out that discourse is often flawed, debasing the role of technology to that of a mediocre mediator:

> *The promise of better fidelity has always been a Hegelian promise of synthesis and supersession—that* this *incarnation of reproducibility will finally capture the essence of some previously unreproduced reality. The perfect mediator would vanish in doing its work. But that moment of perfect correspondence never comes, and, because it never comes, theories of mediation posit sound reproduction as a failure, a sham, and a debasement of a more fundamental live presence.*

[8] In that paper, Burston's argument relies partly on John Corbett's (1990) naïve understanding of the use of "echo" and "compression" in music recording. Both papers are somewhat dated but keep popping up as references in contemporary publications.

Rather than an "original/copy" approach to aesthetic or critical evaluation of sound technologies, a more promising approach is an analysis of the direct effects of transduction processes. Simon Emmerson (2007) describes three *acousmatic* dislocations which are salient features of the use of sound technologies: dislocation of place, time, and causality. These dislocations occur regardless of whether parts of the signal chain are digital or not. Electronic amplification of sound creates a distinctively separate category of sound technology. Sources (a voice or an instrument) are copresent with the loudspeaker that reproduces the amplified sound. The dislocation of time is easily understood in terms of sound recording: ephemeral sound is materialized (in tin, wax, shellac, vinyl, wire, magnetic tape, or a hard drive) in order to be played back at any time in the future, provided the matching playback apparatus can be found. In live sound the dislocation in time is minute: when a sound is transduced by a microphone, a small time shift can be observed. Sound waves travel much faster in the electronic domain than as sound waves in air, almost by a million-fold. The dislocation of place refers to the impossibility of amplifying loudspeakers to be in the same place as the singer or instrumentalist. Loudspeakers adjoining the stage cause a shift in the direction from which an audience perceives the sound (and the difference in time traveled causes yet corresponding time shift).[9] Finally, the sound perceived by the audience is caused by the loudspeaker, often, in the case of pop and rock concerts, drowning out the original acoustic sound produced by a voice or instrument. It is this displacement, the severance of sound and source, that Burston problematizes. The problem, as summed up by Sterne, also surfaces in Raymond Murray Schafer's (1977) and Barry Truax's (1984) rationale for the negative term "schizophonia," which seems to underline the detrimental nature of sound technology processes.

To avoid the pitfalls and challenges of the authenticity debates that regularly emerge (for instance, Moore, 2002; Weisethaunet & Lindberg, 2010), I focus on how amplification, whether using digital elements or not, is a way of producing sound, not an avoidable degradation of a virginal authentic original. Amplification and its consequential dislocations are an essential aspect of music performance, with the exception of the traditional classical music concert in purpose-built concert halls. For instance, consider the awkwardly named "unplugged" concerts, which rely on the use of microphones and loudspeakers, regardless of the name. Rock and pop singers without a (close) microphone are a rarity; the microphonic voice is essential to these (and many other) genres. A notable exception is eloquently demonstrated by the Tiny Desk series of concerts taking place in the offices of the North American public radio provider NPR.[10] The microphone, which also features on the show's logo, is deliberately positioned some distance away from the performers, freeing the vocalists from the restraints of a handheld microphone. As can be seen on the YouTube clips that are released with the broadcasts, the performers are at the same time forced into a sometimes awkward gestural performance without the regular ties to technology in the shape of a microphone and its stand. The microphone is only there to capture and record the acoustic sound for

[9] The ability of our multimodal perception psychology to align differences in hearing and seeing is studied—and experienced—in the ventriloquist effect (Bertelson & Aschersleben, 2003; Connor, 2000).

[10] http://www.npr.org/series/tiny-desk-concerts (viewed July 8, 2014).

broadcast rather than amplification, which is not required in the intimate setting of an office space. Sometimes other instruments such as electric guitars, keyboards, or electric violins are plugged into little amplifiers, simply because they cannot be heard without amplification. A great example is the performance by the band Gogol Bordello in June 2010. Singer Eugene Hutz is on the move and soon outside of the close range of the microphone. By the fifth song only the (plugged) violin and accordion are audible and all the vocals sound far away (the front man is dancing on the desks by that time). An ideologically informed analysis of such a performance situation in terms of sound authenticity or copy/original is hard if not pointless. A discussion of how the sound technology is used, practically or musically, in relation to their workings can advance an understanding of the amplified concert experience. Of interest is the way that performers, mixers, or sound designers deal with the acousmatic dislocations: are they taken for granted or are they utilized in a way that makes the performance stand out? In other words, do the dislocations become performance parameters?

4.6 Music computing and synthesis

In order to support this argument, I need to stipulate some historical steps in the advance of digital music technology, even though this may be familiar territory. Early musical applications of digital technology—computers—are found in academic music research and composition (Chadabe, 1997). The place of computers in academic music practice has become almost central: computational musicology, music retrieval, acousmatic composition, and digital electronic music production are widespread in research and education. In terms of popular music, digital impact came with sampling and increased control over synthesizers. Up until the late 1970s, synthesizers were generally analog and sound synthesis was realized by discreet components (resistors, transistors, capacitors, coils, and so on). By the early 1980s, programming and storage was enhanced by digital hybrid technology while actual synthesis remained analog. Analog synthesizers (with or without digital control, programming, and storage) are still very popular, whether as vintage hardware or new products. Digital sound synthesis, with noticeably different sonic characteristics, became possible with what is known as Frequency Modulation (FM) first available in the renowned Synclavier (1977) and more widely available in Yamaha's popular DX7 synthesizer (1983). The hybrid analog and digital synthesizers became more powerful with the addition of MIDI (Musical Instrument Digital Interface)—a technology which allowed the transfer and storage of digital music parameters (not actual sound but data relating to notes, tempo, and so on). As mentioned earlier, digital computing has a hard time synthesizing the unique analog timbres (although this will surely improve); however, digitally recording the output of such synthesizers will not reduce or diminish the unique analog characteristics. This is an essential difference between digital sound synthesis and digital reproduction of analogs sound through transduction and conversion, as normally found in recording, broadcast, and amplification.

MIDI was put to use in live music to connect different synthesizer modules to a keyboard. It also allowed live performers to play along to pre-produced tracks on a sequencer.[11] Typically a drummer would be performing wearing headphones to hear a backing track or metronome, syncing the whole band to the MIDI-sequencer and the pre-produced material. In one go, a band could perform more complicated arrangements with increased timing accuracy (while saving money on a keyboard player).

The real impact of digital technology on music, recorded as much as live, came with sampling (first available in the revolutionary Australian Fairlight CMI, named after a jetfoil which carried the name of a Sydney suburb). The ability to select a snippet of any existing sound or piece of music (or a barking dog) and use it as the basis to create a new sound appealed to many musicians and music producers but also to academics, who analyzed and critiqued it into becoming a paradigmatic feature of post-modernity. Many (solo) musicians use a number of different sampling/loop and voice processing tools, on the main stages (dub-step-folk star James Blake, voice artist Reggie Watts) but also buskers on the street who use live samples in a loop to create a musical layer which can serve as accompaniment to their own singing or playing. To underline the creative and performative aspects of those tools, some singers perform with a two-microphone setup, which allow singers to demonstrate whether they are singing "normally" through an amplification system or using some form of (digital) processing controlled by themselves (instead of leaving that control to an the agent at the mixing desk).[12] Once the compact disc (CD) became available commercially (1982/3), it announced the digitization of both music production and consumption, and this has accelerated due to the more recent availability of fast and reliable Internet connections, miniature portable music players, tablets, and smartphones.

4.7 Remote digital tools

The twenty-first-century miniaturization of personal computing and telecom devices (tables, smartphones, and hybrid laptops) has not left the live sound practice untouched. Most digital live sound platforms allow full remote control via brand specific applications or "apps." The obvious advantage is that the mixing engineers can leave their position behind a desk and verify the consistency of the mix or adjust loudspeaker system settings in different positions. At pop concerts and festivals, the mixer or system engineer can now be spotted roaming the venue or grounds, which not only increases that person's engagement with the audience experience but also removes the formality of the technical setup, opening up interaction with individual audience members, whether desirable or not. Although there are some obvious advantages, leaving the mixing position with a touch screen remote greatly reduces the tactility and immediacy of control that were valued so highly in the analog mixing desk.

The central machine in the sound engineering chain, the mixing desk, has now become a DAW very similar to those found in most recording studios. The control surface and interconnections are tailored to performance sound use, but the core is

[11] A sequencer records music data such as MIDI so it can be edited and played back later.

[12] For instance, Bon Iver can be seen and heard performing with two microphones and a voice processor in YouTube footage from his 2012 tour.

a powerful computer optimized for Digital Signal Processing (DSP). The processes are generally identical to studio mixing with the exception of editing—cutting and pasting—and rearranging of a song or smaller elements. Increasing processing power is slowly adding automated tasks to the digital mixer. It is not a common tool in pop and rock amplification, but in public address systems when multiple microphones (e.g. for a debate or a conference) are required, technical improvements can be achieved (e.g. system gain and unintentional (comb-) filtering as a consequence of crosstalk) (Clifford & Reiss, 2011).[13] Auto mixing, as that process is known, and "feedback killers" are making their way into the digital mixing desk and will increasingly aid live sound engineers. Remote controllers and digital tools supporting small improvements in technical sound quality improve concert outcomes by very small increments, but they have a limited impact on how music is made let alone helping to generate whole new musical genres, which was the case with sampling. These improvements support and perhaps help reinforce the false notion that the whole amplification layer of transduction, conversion, processing conversion, and transduction is transparent.

With the introduction of Digidesign's Venue in 2005, live mixing consoles became closer to the DAW of the recording studio. Digidesign supplies a recording studio software suite called Protools (and related hardware such as control surfaces and digital converters), which at that time was dominant in the studio and home recording market. With their live mixing control surface, essentially a mixing desk, they were the first to enable the use of plug-ins in live sound, generally the same plug-ins as used in the studio. Simon Frith (2002, p. 286) has argued that rock music is essentially a recorded music that is constructed in the studio, and that is where the art of performance takes place, with the live performance merely a copy. Although this reductionist viewpoint appears to posit that a concert is just the music, nothing more, nothing less, the newly reaffirmed overlap between live and recording technology appears to support this point. With the ability to use plug-ins on a digital live desk, live mixing has come one step closer to working in the studio, with the unique possibilities in the studio of dubbing, editing, cutting, pasting, and rearranging over time as the salient exceptions.

4.8 Digital magic

Digital tools changed the world of music, but I shall argue here that its real power does not surface in recorded music. The production process is severed from what the consumer hears; all the different reiterations, mixes, preselections remain in the studio, including all the processes of filtering, compressing, reverberating, bit crunching, and amp-simulation. It is, however, in the realm of live music, in the real-time domain that the power of digital computing becomes overwhelmingly apparent. The most obvious example of that power—pitch processing of vocals—is also the site for much debate around questions of authenticity. The possibility to change a singer's pitch in real-time became available as a software plug-in in 1997 and as a hardware unit in 2002 (both

[13] Crosstalk refers to the fact that one microphone never just picks up the one intended sound source, there is always "bleed" from other instruments.

made the company Antares). The AVP-1 hardware unit quickly found its way into the equipment racks of live mixers. With the introduction of plug-ins on live mixing desks, pitch correction and the "Cher effect" became available at the touch of a button.

As I have argued above, digital technology is used very successfully in replicating analog technologies. This goes one step further in cases where technology replicates not just older technologies, but absent or deceased artists. In popular music, performers have been playing along prerecorded tracks, or pretending to play, but accompanying prerecorded vocals appears to be rare. In recent years, not so much made possible but certainly made easier by digital technology, a few of such examples can be identified. The appearance of Tupac at the 2012 Coachella festival by means of a visual effect called Pepper's Ghost is possibly the most famous occurrence.[14] The visual display moved and mimed along to both Tupac's original recordings and apparently also used a synthesized version of his voice. A few years before that, in 2009, the French *Orchestre National de Jazz* toured performing an album recorded with British singer Robert Wyatt.[15] The singer was not able to join the band on that tour so they performed without him, playing along to his prerecorded vocals and keeping in sync by a click track. Songs featuring a disembodied singer were alternated with live-on-stage guest vocalists, emphasizing the oddity, and experiential complexity, of a disembodied performance.

Completely dependent on the digital and taking the disembodied voice one step further are performances by "virtual idols," accompanied by human instrumentalists. Very popular in Japan but also globally is virtual pop idol Miku Hatsune, whose singing is brought to life by voice synthesis software.[16] Her original, or perhaps initial, "looks" appeared just once, on the package of a commercial vocal synthesizer package. Soon it became the rage to create pop songs and video clips using that particular synthesized voice and animations of the idol's image (Hamasaki, Takeda, & Nishimura, 2008; Kenmochi 2010).[17] Fascinatingly, using the Pepper's Ghost effect, the animated character started performing live, backed by a band with actual human musicians (whether they really played live seems less relevant in this context, but it sounds like they do) with a first performance in August 2009.[18] In footage from a concert in Los Angeles (July 2011), the singer's animation is projected on stage, with a token microphone, backed by a band with a string section. The addition of the acoustic string instruments puts extra emphasis on the contradiction between a virtual vocalist and a human band, as if stronger roots in the music performance history were desired.

[14] Pepper's Ghost is an optical illusion discovered in the nineteenth century (Nickell, 2005, p. 288). Multi projector screen-less animation is sometimes mistakenly referred to as a hologram, a technology that has not been realized at this point in time. Entertainment technologist John Huntington (2012) asserts in a blog post that even though holograms can be seen at work in *Star Wars*, we'll have light sabers (weaponry of choice in the *Star Wars* movies) before we have holograms!

[15] The album from 2009 was entitled *Around Robert Wyatt* on Bee Jazz (BEE 030).

[16] Yamaha's "Vocaloid2" singing voice synthesis software.

[17] In May 2010, an album with tracks by different users (i.e. of this particular software) titled *Exit Tunes Presents Vocalogenesis feat. Hatsune Miku* topped the Japanese (Oricon) charts.

[18] There are many clips of the concert available on the Internet. I refer here to the concerts in Los Angeles in 2011 in particular. The string section was left out in later shows.

4.9 Conclusion

Slowly but surely, digital technology has taken over much of the audio chain between microphone input and loudspeaker output. As demonstrated by the possibility of real-time (vocal) pitch correction, the creative opportunities of powerful computing are massive. However, in general and at this moment in time, the digital emulates the trusted and reliable analog sound engineering processes and the influence of the digital on live sound does not have the same impact that it continues to have on recorded music. In pop and rock, the ability to mimic works created in the studio remains an attractive alternative to exploration and experimentation with the previously unheard-of processing power of the digital signal chain.

The genesis of digital audio in live music production shows that large encompassing narratives and philosophies of new media are fraught with the pitfalls of aesthetic objectification. It is not the (digital) process that provides us with a categorical framework for critiquing and analysis. What matters is how such processes are used, what choices are made, and how debates are informed by such choices. The three acousmatic dislocations are salient features of sound technology that inform, enhance, or frustrate our sonic experience. Digital conversion and signal processes take place within the audible boundaries of the dislocation of time. That time frame allows for the digital to either go unnoticed or to facilitate the auditory hyperbole of autotune and similar, previously unheard, processes. Digital technology, although a facilitator of the previously impossible, disappears as a distinct element in the larger context of the popular music concert.

References

Auslander, P. (2008). *Liveness: performance in a mediatized culture* (2nd). London, New York: Routledge.

Becker-Foss, C., Flock, S., Helmut, J., Langen, C., Werwein, M., & Wittek, H. (2010). *White paper: digital microphones and AES42*. Retrieved July 1, 2014 from http://www.hauptmikrofon.de/doc/WhitePaperE_AES42_v21_May2010.PDF.

Bertelson, P. & Aschersleben, G. (2003). Temporal ventriloquism: Crossmodal interaction on the time dimension 1. Evidence from auditory-visual temporal order judgment. *International Journal of Psychophysiology*, 50, 147–155.

Blesser, B., & Lee, F. (1971). An audio delay system using digital technology. *Journal of the Audio Engineering Society*, 19(5), 393–397.

Blesser, B., & Salter, L.-R. (2006). *Spaces speak, are you listening?: experiencing aural architecture*. Cambridge, MA: MIT Press.

Burston, J. (1998). Theatre space as virtual place: audio technology, the reconfigured singing body, and the megamusical. *Popular Music*, 17(2), 20–218.

Chadabe, J. (1997). *Electric sound: the past and promise of electronic music*. Upper Saddle River, NJ: Prentice Hall.

Clifford, A. & Reiss, J. (2011). Microphone interference reduction in live sound. In *Paper presented at the proceedings of the 14th international conference on digital audio effects (DAFx-11)*.

Connor, S. (2000). *Dumbstruck: a cultural history of ventriloquism*. Oxford, New York: Oxford University Press.

Corbett, J. (1990). Free, single, and disengaged: listening pleasure and the popular music object. *October*, 54(Autumn), 79–101.

Emmerson, S. (2007). *Living electronic music*. Aldershot: Ashgate.

Frere-Jones, S. (2008). *The gerbil's revenge: Autotune corrects a singer's pitch. It also distorts—a grand tradition in pop*. New York: The New Yorker June 9.

Hamasaki, M., Takeda, H., & Nishimura, T. (2008). Network Analysis of Massively Collaborative Creation of Multimedia Contents Case Study of Hatsune Miku videos on Nico Nico Douga. Paper presented at the uxTV'08. Silicon Valley, California, USA.

Holt, F. (2010). The economy of live music in the digital age. *European Journal of Cultural Studies*, 13(2), 243–261.

Huntington, J. (2011). *Does star quad microphone cable sound better? Let's find out!*. Retrieved from http://controlgeek.net/blog/2011/2/27/does-star-quad-microphone-cable-sound-better-lets-find-out.html.

Huntington, J. (2012). *It's not a f*cking hologram part II*. Blog Retrieved from http://www.controlgeek.net/blog/2012/4/17/its-not-a-fcking-hologram-part-ii.html.

Kenmochi, H. (2010). VOCALOID and Hatsune Miku phenomenon in Japan Paper presented at the InterSinging 2010. First Interdisciplinary Workshop on Singing Voice, Tokyo, Japan.

McCutchen, B. (1927). 1642040. Free patents online: U. p. office.

Moore, A. (2002). Authenticity as authentication. *Popular Music*, 21(02), 209–223. http://dx.doi.org/10.1017/S0261143002002131.

Mortimer, J. H., Nosko, C., & Sorensen, A. (2012). Supply responses to digital distribution: Recorded music and live performances. *Information Economics and Policy*, 24(1), 3–14.

Nickell, J. (2005). *Secrets of the sideshows*. Kentucky: University Press of Kentucky.

Rogers, J. (2013). *The death and life of the music industry in the digital age*. New York: Bloomsbury Academic.

Schafer, R. M. (1977). *The soundscape: Our sonic environment and the tuning of the world*. Rochester, VT: Destiny Books.

Sterne, J. (2003). *The audible past: cultural origins of sound reproduction*. Durham: Duke University Press.

Sterne, J. (2006). The mp3 as cultural artifact. *New Media and Society*, 8(5), 825–842.

Théberge, P. (2001). Plugged in. In S. Frith, W. Straw, & J. Street (Eds), *The Cambridge companion to pop and rock*. Cambridge: Cambridge University Press.

Truax, B. (1984). *Acoustic communication*. Westport, CN: Ablex Pub. Corp.

Wakin, D. J. (2009). *The frigid fingers were live, but the music wasn't*. New York: New York Times. Retrieved from http://www.nytimes.com/2009/01/23/arts/music/23band.html?_r=0.

Weisethaunet, H. & Lindberg, U. (2010). Authenticity revisited: The rock critic and the changing real. *Popular Music and Society*, 33(4), 465–485. http://dx.doi.org/10.1080/03007761003694225.

Wurtzler, S. (1992). She sang live, but the microphone was turned off: the live, the recorded, and the subject of representation. In R. Altman (Ed.), *Sound theory, sound practice* (pp. 291). New York: Routledge.

Live or Memorex? Changing perceptions of music practices

5

S. Mallinder

5.1 Introduction

The ritual of music has been diminished. The depth to which we experience music has been lessened to accommodate the volume of new experiences

(Joe Morgan—musician/producer)

In consideration of an increasingly complex sonic ecology, one in which players, users, and stakeholders shift constantly between tangible and virtual worlds, the very idea of what constitutes "live" in such mediated conditions has become problematic. Understandings of place, space, and temporality which underpin "liveness" in an analog world have become distorted in a digital domain. "Live" implies a capturing of "the moment," the experience, the emotive context, and importantly suggests authenticity in music and sound. As we have moved into a largely digital ecology, important changes have resulted in music production but even more significant changes to music's transmission, specifically how the studio or event performance is recorded and mediated. Reduced to digital information, which is frequently repurposed and transmitted through online platforms and mobile technologies, understandings of liveness and authenticity, shaped in an analog world, have been challenged. This questions not merely music's commodification, but importantly whether music, as a tangible product, continues to underpin meaning. Is music no longer a noun but rather a verb? As digital information, online sound and image can be considered as perpetually active, stimulating a range of activities and experiences in which we are all dynamically engaged. *Live or Memorex?* positions "liveness" within this discourse. Currently the importance of "what" is being created is becoming superseded by the significance of not only "how" it is being produced but also being transmitted, consumed, reconfigured, and shared. The malleability of digital sound has resulted in users, once merely consumers, now adept at reshaping information to become ancillary producers, making the creative process a dynamic and progressive. It is against this backdrop of a continual "switched-on," active, state that the chapter challenges not only what constitutes live but also what we regard as an authentic creation or experience in this complex interface of analog and digital.

The definition of "live" applied in the chapter is set against this backdrop of mass digitization of sound; this process has created complex interpretations of the meaning of "liveness." Initially this is considered in more conventional auditory terms, where "live" is fixed through performance—how it is captured, packaged, and transmitted. Specifically to what extent have artists (in the studio or gig) accommodated, or rejected, the loss of grit and tangibility for the immediacy of digital, and how does this impact upon the audience's perception of music, as performance and in consumption? How live is live? The second, more metaphysical, interpretation is prompted by the shift to sound as active digital information, constantly "live," this sonic information is continually being configured, transmitted, reshaped, and moved on. Through online platforms, mobile technologies, and digital delivery systems, artists and consumers alike are animating and transmitting this sonic information to potential global audiences—nothing is new, nothing is lost, and everything becomes transformed.

While we acknowledge the extent to which the actual delivery systems themselves are shaping change, music, as a creative process, continues to position artists as central to our grasp of its meaning and significance. Systemic considerations aside, great store is placed in how artists and musicians, as primary users, articulate changing practices and experiences. Considering this, *Live or Memorex?* seeks to capture current perceptions. By posing a series of simple questions, allowing respondents the opportunity to reflect and expand on their perceptions, 30 "music" makers and players were asked what they felt had been lost or gained in the shift from analog to predominantly digital modalities in sound and music, particularly what constitutes live, real-time, authentic creativity, and experience.

This chapter extends Christopher Small's (1998) definition of "musicking" where active engagement in music in "any capacity" (p. 9) recognizes a wider cultural participation, where even our perception of what constitutes the artist, or producer, has become complex. In an online ecology we are no longer exclusively producers or consumers, but all actively involved in the creative process, capturing, adapting, and disseminating: "producers" (Bruns, 2007), active participants in a fractal and accelerating online world. As the artifact has become increasingly detached from the music in the download economy, the underlying consideration must be to question whether music is a "thing". Should we consider music online merely a component of a much wider service industry, switched on and off at will? One which has become the medium of choice for storing and exchanging information in all its forms, a productless default activity for a work-leisure ecology. One in which we are all live participants, in Nicholas Carr's (2008) words: "the preferred means of entertaining informing, and expressing ourselves" (p. 124). In separating music from the object, and, indeed, the untethering of our past preoccupation with music products, we can begin to consider music in its essential role of cultural and social agent forever experiencing and transmitting in the moment.

Evidence tells us that music inherently encourages participation, collaboration, and sharing. The final consideration is how the traditional perception of "live" music, specifically the idea that it is through live performance, that the artist-audience relationship is maintained in a digital information age. It is seemingly through the visceral moment, or "event" experience, that some effective economic model and artistic centrality can be sustained. However, the Internet, as a system, and our sharing practices have also impacted in this experiencing of the moment.

5.2 Methodology

Building upon direct interviews and an online questionnaire, *Live or Memorex?* draws on the views and reflections of the respondents from Europe, the USA, and Australia. The questions, which asked about the key themes of "listening," "making," "performing," and "playing" of music and sound, were designed to be inclusive to enable the respondents to reflect and consider the wider implications of the analog to digital discourse:[1]

> *What do you feel has been lost as we have moved to predominantly digital forms of recording? What has been gained?*
> *What do you feel has been lost as we have moved to predominantly digital forms of playing back/listening to sound? What has been gained?*
> *What do you feel has been lost as we have moved to predominantly digital forms of performance/playing live/DJ-ing? What has been gained?*

These observations are aligned with wider perceptions from academics, musicians, and cultural observers, together with understandings of the author—himself a producer for over 30 years. The responses, from the largely electronic musicians, producers, and DJs (many choosing anonymity), offered an opportunity for them to share their thoughts on the shifts from predominantly analog to digital audio forms and practices.

The chapter's themes address the sense of loss felt in move from analog processes to more abstracted use of digital sound, which has prompted a growth in nostalgia and the fetishization of past music cultures. The increased archiving and massification of sound online has produced a surfeit which has undermined music's exchange value but widened its functionality and raised its use value. Drawing on this change, the chapter looks to how the liquidity of sound has transformed our association with music, from relatively passive consumers to active users. Sound is live and transferable information. In consideration of the live performance, the chapter addresses how our relationship with events and gigs, as artists and audiences, has been reshaped by technology. The final theme draws on the underlying tension evident in many of the respondents' comments—the loss of dynamic in our shift to predominantly digital ways of making and presenting music. Authenticity or utility, it is an ongoing discourse.

5.3 The loss of the tangible—capturing the moment 1

> *The tension between the knowledge that records are inanimate objects and the fact that they facilitate profoundly human experiences*
>
> *Chivers Yochim & Biddinger (2008)*

Many of the artists' responses implied that the loss of tangibility in the transition to digital had the greatest impact on how sound was perceived. Since the advent of the

[1] All the responses from musicians, DJs, producers, and sound-recordists have been archived and can be accessed at *Live or Memorex? Artists' and Producers' Perceptions of Changing Music Practices*: liveormemorex.blogspot.com.

recording, the authentic, live performance has been captured in tangible form. As sound became reduced to its pure abstract state, it was the forfeiting of the attendant forms, the packaging, text, and visual presentation for so long a significant part of popular music that appeared to be the most important consideration. Understandably this sacrifice of product, the "thing" we hold, show, and share, is deeply ingrained. Not merely the loss of a readily bought and exchanged product, it is, as Chivers et al. suggest, the severing of the connection between live emotive content and the listener. Mourning the loss of analog cultures is interwoven with memory, authenticity, and sense-of-self, necessitating a rethinking of perceptions of ourselves and others, and requiring new constructions of identity and association. Sound, moving fluidly online, has augmented but not replaced past constructions of a connection and self. Many artists' and producers' responses highlight this sense of tension between the loss of past tangibility and newer means of access and use of recorded sound. In the repositioning of music's "content" and "form," respondents considered there was no longer:

> *[the] Satisfaction of being able to hold what your money has purchased, to know it's yours and not some form of legal license to listen to only on some devices dictated by lawyers and politicians.*
>
> *(Respondent—producer)*

> *A sense of occasion ... the thrill of the chase getting hold of things.*
>
> *(Respondent—producer)*

> *Record sleeves for the most part. I remember handling them and reading them as though they were religious artifacts.*
>
> *(Respondent—musician)*

Our relationship with past technologies and processes is encapsulated through vinyl records more than any other form. Music consumers' connection with records does not merely romanticize the past, but is a means of articulating an abstract relationship between technology and humanity (Chivers Yochim & Biddinger, 2008, p. 185), invoking the past in a very idealized way. This has created a crisis with music's increased liquidity and file-sharing. The free movement of digital sound online has challenged our understanding of music as something tangible to being repositioned as a process, or practice. There is a sense that holding a CD or vinyl record offers something real, that sound is *physical* and "*alive*" (ibid, p. 189), not just an illusion, making us believe we are actually holding the live recording itself:

> *A physical object that sang to you.*
>
> *(Respondent—producer)*

Music differs from other art forms where it is possible to differentiate content from form; here the creative output is held within the object itself. Those anchored to past music cultures must confront the idea that "either music has dematerialized, or its materiality exists on a different scale" (Sterne, 2012, p. 186). There is a sense that the loss of physicality brings with it a loss of connection and community through a shared appreciation not only of the form but also of the process, "the moving parts of a turntable and the ability to see what's going on allow you to participate more in the music—there's a more participatory nature to listening to vinyl than listening to mp3s or CDs" (Chivers Yochim & Biddinger, 2008, p. 190). Sound, though still malleable, was no longer tactile.

The digital recording process has itself displaced the role of merely capturing the live performance to one of on-screen sound manipulation. The technology itself has moved away from past professional benchmarks built upon

> *Old studios with amazing microphone selections and reams of analogue gear.*
>
> *(Steve Cobby, producer and musician)*

This denotes a greater emphasis on direct input and "on-screen" post-production with less physical and live recording required. For sound recordist Chris Watson, many of the field recoding technologies built in important processes that were in danger of being forgotten:

> *Playing back and listening to my analogue recordings is a real time experience through a linear process. Working with my old analogue recordings I tend to listen through tracks without the interruption of stopping to rewind or fast forward as this is an imprecise operation where time is often wasted and the flow, pace and feel of a recording may be broken. I feel I sometimes lose this careful listening and consideration time with a move to digital.*
>
> *(Chris Watson, sound recordist)*

In broader cultural terms, Simon Reynolds' analysis of how we have become absorbed in popular culture's past this sense of loss has been an important part of how the fanaticism with recorded sound is framed, stressing that there is "an antagonism to the present day, the belief that something's been lost" (2011, p. 205). For many, this merely underlines the music industry's cynical grab for profit, happy to exploit new platforms and mediums as a means of extracting every drop from their catalog. For many consumers, the appropriate response was to reject this continual construction of the "new" through technology by proudly cementing one's position in a past cultural period. As Reynolds observed, "if time has become annexed by capitalism's cynical cycles of product shifting, one way to resist that is to reject temporality all together. The revivalist does so by fixating on one era" (2011, p. 201). Clearly if cultural time were now merely a construct, we could confidently say that the future did not exist and we could happily fixate on period of our own choosing, frequently one in which musicianship and performance were identifiable and revered. Looking backward to an archived and subsequently imitated past has simply become a part of the nature of popular culture.

Understandably, this sense of loss has been driven by, but also promoted, a high level of nostalgia and fetishization drawing upon an idealized, mythologized heritage, manifested in a number of ways through our replication of past technologies and cultures, but also through our tendency to ingrain older mediums, vinyl, and cassettes, with almost mythical power. The processes of analog recording, the sheer physicality of the objects themselves enables them to capture the live, emotive, content of music. This is not dissimilar to the much-vaunted idea of photographs capturing the soul, "when people heard voices over a phonograph, they often noted how the speaker's *spirit* seemed to be present, as though actually residing in the machine itself" (Chivers Yochim & Biddinger, 2008, p. 185). In recent years there has been a revisiting of Derrida's (1994) twisting of ontology to "hauntology" most effectively in David Toop's (2004) investigation into sound, memory and emotional loss. In psychogeography where "place" captures and reveals us, our past is sealed in these bygone cultural artifacts, most effectively it would seem in vinyl records, which can subsequently be released into the digital world. These sounds, echoes of a live past, represent an analog past that has been archived for our wonder.

5.4 Plus ça change—capturing the moment 2

> *When John D. Smoot, an engineer for the European company Odeon, carted primitive recording equipment to the Indonesian archipelago in 1904 to record the gamelan orchestras, local musicians were perplexed. Why copy a performance? The popular local tunes that circulated in their villages had a half-life of a few weeks. Why would anyone want to listen to a stale rendition of an obsolete piece when it was so easy to get fresh music?*
>
> *Kelly (2002)*

If recording is central to the music narrative, a paradigm shift in production technology came in the form of the digital sampler enabling sounds to be actually cloned, rather than merely analogously copied or simulated. By reducing sound to a binary code, it has been possible for popular culture's past, those limitless archives of live recordings, not merely to be imitated, but replicated. As a consequence, music's past, its reserve of recorded live music, became "a gigantic archive, virtually every recess of the past is accessible to us" (Reynolds, 2011, p. 200), and importantly reworked into the present as a cultural time tapestry. The ease with which this can be achieved has made the process, and often simplistic results, passé for many producers. Sampling, it would seem, has become a nuanced technique. The interviews and survey responses suggest that producers are accepting of this, a simple culture of acquiescence. Sampling as a process, a technology, or a concept was not directly referred to once. The sample, once offering a culture of production with infinite possibilities, of copyright lawlessness or injunctions, of new hybridization, is now simply an accepted part of popular music. As Kevin Kelly noted, "there is no music made today that has not been shaped by the fact of recording and duplication. In fact, the ability to copy music has been deeply disruptive ever since the invention of the gramophone" (2002). Indeed, music cultures have been continually adapting to the processes of copying (and subsequently copyright); Kelly notes that in Calcutta in 1902, only two decades after the phonograph was invented, he found that Indian musicians were already learning to imitate recorded music and lamented that there was "no traditional music left to record" (ibid). However, the availability of limitless clone sounds has created not merely liquidity with free movement of digital information but, as a consequence, began the process of massification of music.

Many respondents, as significant users of this online surfeit, had no issue with this availability of live sounds but were immersed in technology that processed, recorded, and played the music. A number responded underlining the point that:

Nothing is lost.

(Respondent—producer)

It's all there if you want it.

(Respondent—DJ)

And significantly the misconception that one system was being replaced another, was unfounded.

I don't see a problem of either—or I just use anything available that works for me. It seems ridiculous to be in one camp or another … it's just a tool, use it as such.

(Respondent—producer)

The key consideration is the impact of this liquidity—as downloading, file-sharing, bit torrents, and instant transferability have made mp3s the overriding form—is that with digitization, music has reverted to its preconsumer role of social and cultural service rather than a generation of "product." Music has gone from being a noun to a verb once again. Sound files have become live and dynamic components of an ongoing creative process. Digitization has changed behaviors; players of digitized sound are not consumers but, in accepted parlance, users (Poster, 2004, p. 417), conforming less to past cultural norms than to the protocols of the Internet. The movement of sound files online adheres less to the exchange values of consumer capitalism and more to principles of free movement and exchange of information of the Internet.

To understand the transformation of live sound in the shift from analog to digital, we must consider the dissemination of sound as being the principle driver above the preservation of the product's exchange value. In the push to maximize public access to the greatest volume of recorded sound, the music industry failed to see the irony that it was nurturing the seeds of its own demise. In the push, during the 1980s, to digitize much of their back catalogue the music industry, was largely blind to digital music's inherent functionality. The ease of producing faultless duplication when sound was encoded as data would become the industry's "Achilles Heel" (Reynolds, 2011, p.68) as music could be copied, moved and shared cheaply and without difficulty. The ease with which sound was replicated coupled with a highly networked environment has shaped current music culture. Chris Anderson's (2009) observation of this "free" economy is exacerbated by digital natives who "[have] grown up online simply assuming that everything digital is free" (p. 10). Unlike natural resources, digital resources can never be used up: nothing new, nothing lost, everything transformed. As Poster comments, "digitization also means the object is more difficult to destroy since it exists on the Internet" (2005); as a consequence, sounds move ad infinitum in the online ecology of supply and demand, locked in an eternal embrace.

5.5 Liquid sounds—disseminating the experience

Telephony and the peculiar characteristics of its infrastructure are central to the sound of most audio technologies over the past 130 years.

Jonathon Sterne (2012, pp. 2–3)

Changes to how to engage with audio have been complemented by how we access, share, and view images, photographs, film, and video, through laptops, tablets, and mobile devices. Widely available and affordable technology has made "liveness" as captured experiences much easier to create and upload to sites such as Flickr, Vimeo, and YouTube, particularly when we acknowledge the role played by social networking. Mp3s have transformed our use and application of sound. In translating sound to binary data, the mp3 selected key information and junked superfluous information—outside our auditory requirements—producing soundfiles which are incredibly small when compared to the .wav files that we find on compact discs. This can be considered a triumph for compression and its suitability to the the rapid transfer and sharing of information. The compressed files requiring substantially less bandwidth through which to move and storage space when downloaded. For this reason, Sterne emphasizes the need to consider the shift to digital cultures as being "at least as telephonic as it is phonographic or digital" (2012, p. 3) when compared to "the usual, more aestheticized subjects of twentieth—century media history such as cinema, television, sound recording, radio, print and computers" (ibid, pp. 2–3), and it should not be overlooked.

The activation and animation of digital information, supported by fluid movement of files online, have reshaped our relationship with music. The cultural object loses its fixity and the "consumer" becomes not a user but a creator (Poster, 2004, p. 418). In changing the user's role to that of active participant, the expectations of that engagement have shifted, "effectively treating music as information rather than an immersive sonic experience" (Reynolds, 2011, p. 61). As a consequence of massification, many listeners engagement with music was no longer characterized by the deep emotional commitment they once experienced. This view reinforces the belief that for convenience and accessibility, we have traded quantity against quality in our digital music relationship. Music, once regarded as a highly valued commodity, now readily downloaded, is simply another commodity that is available in abundance through direct access. The process has become privatized; engagement has become wide but not deep. Nevertheless, this engagement has become in real-time live and dynamic.

For musicians, there is a considerable advantage in this flexibility and ease of access. Responses suggested that practices have become enhanced by this active engagement:

> *Music has never been so portable.*
>
> *(Respondent—musician)*

> *The ability to realise ideas more efficiently and effectively … convenience (in a good way) and possibilities.*
>
> *(Respondent—producer)*

> *I have almost instant access to any of my digital recordings and can sequence them quickly in any order.*
>
> *(Chris Watson, sound recordist)*

And quite simply:

> *Control.*
>
> *(Respondent—producer)*

In consideration of flexibility in performance, one respondent captured the changing perception of "liveness" in the digital domain:

> *It is now possible to be a one-man act with a laptop and fill a venue. You don't need a band.*
> *(Respondent—musician)*

In an interview, one producer commented upon how this new engagement supported its creative application by opening up spaces for performance and recording:

> *Access to the recording process has been massively opened up, allowing more people the opportunity to explore music-making. The portability of recording equipment has also been of great benefit I think, the ability to choose your recording space and location has also opened up great possibilities for the musician.*
> *(Phil Winter—musician)*

Past notions of space have become transformed both in respect of flexibility of recording, where the traditional idea of the "studio" has become largely meaningless in laptop production, and of performance, where access to functional space and amplification are the only basic requirements. Software has made previous bulky and expensive analog hardware—compressors, delays, reverbs, multichannel routing, and even keyboards and synthesizers—available on-screen which, with the miniaturization of sound systems, has reduced studios to a virtual, on-screen, state. Producers embraced this flexibility, commenting that it enabled them to have much greater flexibility, and effective engagement:

> *The ability to work on multiple amounts of music at the same time.*
> *(Respondent—producer)*
> *The ability to realise ideas more efficiently and effectively.*
> *(Respondent—producer)*

For DJs, who would argue that their role is a live and dynamic manipulation of recorded sound, the shift to digital files, with the concomitant dematerializing of that sound, has been advantageous in terms of flexibility and portability. The use of synchronizing systems, the most widely used being "Traktor,"[2] facilitates the controlling of sound-files enabling DJs to integrate external players, turntables, and compact disc-players, or now, most commonly, the simple use of digital libraries on-screen for mixing. Respondents alluded to the impact of this shift in terms of:

> *[The] ease of use and portability.*
> *(Respondent—DJ)*

> *[The] ease of use, bigger music libraries.*
> *(Respondent—DJ)*

[2] Traktor is DJ software, developed by Native Instruments, which runs on a multi-tracking system allowing external inputs, turntables and CD players as well as internal onscreen sound-files -to be synchronized with the capacity to shift tempo and control pitch tempo is commonly used by DJs. See http://www.native-instruments.com/en/products/traktor/traktor-for-ios/traktor-dj/.

> *In DJ-ing the bulk of vinyl is gone, an artist can jump on a jet plane with a laptop and that's all he needs.*
>
> *(Respondent—DJ)*

The consensus view is that the digitization of recorded sound has transformed the notion of "liveness" and performance for the artist and the expectations of the audience.

5.6 Keeping it real—live and digital

> *Live music is a product of broad social and cultural transformations in modernity.*
>
> *Mark Poster (2005)*

If any addenda could be included to Mark Poster's analysis, it would be to acknowledge "economic" and "technological" transformations. Poster considers the term "live" as a performance that is not preproduced in a studio and mediated via a playback device. Performance is defined as "an authentic practice by contrasting creative musicianship with the recording as a 'dead' object" (2005, p. 245). In past readings this has posited "live" as a face-to-face encounter between performer and audience, a fixed immobile episode. However, as noted in the DJ's perception of his role above, respondents articulate how has been reshaped in recent times to incorporate technologically mediated performances. Digital media has changed this communication dynamic in terms of space and time. For many consumers, music's power is still anchored to it being a performance, a visceral process. The live event maintains this authentic practice, but the tools of the performance and perhaps to a greater extent the means of dissemination and access online have broadened the meaning of live.

The ubiquity of mobile technology has transformed live events for both artists and fans. With mobile phones elevated, scanning the room, the activities of fans has begun to supersede the activity of the musicians on the stage. Similarly, bands themselves use Internet technology to support wider networking, participating in dialog, and actively encouraging fandom. Lucy Bennett (2012) acknowledges this changing phenomenon which has begun both to extend the limits of the performance space and also to reshape our understanding of the live experience by encouraging practices which, "[work] to re-appropriate ideas of immersion in 'liveness'" (p. 545). A good example of this supplementary digital impact has been the series of Kraftwerk shows at Tate Modern Turbine Hall in February 2013. The rapid and extensive dissemination of information and online streams, via YouTube links circulated through social networks, almost immediately after the performances, gave evidence of an impact far beyond the limited capacity audience on the night. Within the space itself, gigs frequently use mobile technology and social networking within the space to locate friends and beyond to those not attending through images, streams, and comments. Concomitantly, artists themselves use Internet technology to support this wider networking and participate in dialog offering set-lists, gig updates, forums, and official live streaming. Bennett notes:

> *Twitter and Facebook [have] not only allowed fans to find and connect with each other at shows, but also to tweet concert set-lists and other information as they happen, thereby allowing non-attendees around the world to feel part of the event ... online tools are involving individuals who are not physically present at the show, seemingly incorporating them into the real-time "live" experience.*
>
> *(2012, p. 545)*

Respondents differed in their view of digital performance, much of which in electronic music has perhaps eroded the visceral nature of performance. A number of producers and artists believed:

> *[The loss of] spectacle, seeing somebody hunched over a laptop is never very interesting.*
>
> *(Respondent—musician)*

And fearing its impact on real performance:

> *They seem to be having more fun than the poor guy/girl struggling with a crashed Traktor.*
>
> *(Respondent—musician)*

Aware of the shortcomings of digital performance regarding malleability and finessing of sound, Chris Watson utilized an analog mixing-desk to offer a more hands-on element to his performances, noting:

> *Performing with analogue equipment was a very tactile experience manipulating the control surfaces of electronic instruments. Digital instrumentation tends to be screen and software based which can distance the performer from the controls.*

However, the caveat seems to be that working in sound, the visual component can be overstated and sonic condition should prevail. Watson, alluding to the availability of choice and flexibility in the live arena, added:

> *The joy of working with digital files in a performance environment is the ability to have many channels and sound sources to work with in a multi-channel system.*

The ubiquity of the laptop in digital performance, its inherent value, and creative potential in a live context was highlighted by musician Phil Winter:

> *The laptop seems to have set up home on most stages, whether you can see it or not, this has of course had a massive impact on the possibilities of live sound which has been great. As digital technology moves forward I'm sure the interaction between musician and computer will expand.*

From the perspective of the audience, what constitutes "live" has equally been inverted; music forms part of a wider online entertainment industry that functions as much through Internet platforms and social media as through the traditionally spaced and timed performer–audience equation. Nevertheless, this is not merely a product of the digital age. Radio and television have posited the live performance in the moment, key popular cultural milestones shared by millions. From Elvis on the Ed Sullivan Show to the Sex Pistols on Bill Grundy, as Simon Reynolds observes, "pop music's essence is of the 'event' as permanent, subject to endless repetition. The moment becomes and monument" (2011, p. xxxvi). Our current capacity to interact and share this moment recalibrates "live" as an almost simulated event absorbed into a rich online archive experienced outside the previous limitations of time and place.

5.7 Dubstep or busted speakers? Changing auditory practices

> *Dirt, grit, filth and the gas driven, diamond-sharded crackle of the elements. I clearly remember the day I [heard] my first CD. I was impressed by how clean and crisp it sounded but also saddened and disappointed that it lacked the bollocks of my mix-tapes.*
>
> *(Respondent—musician)*

The seeming loss of the sonic dynamic in music that has accompanied the shift to digital can be considered, correctly or not, as eroding music's "liveness." Music's authenticity is fixed in its sonic texture. Regardless of the writing, arrangement, and performance, the sound quality, dynamic range, and frequency response, specifically the relationship between the recorded sound and the output sound, are factors fundamental to audio culture. Mediated by tools of production, transmission, and reception, or more simply how the sounds are made, recorded, and heard by the listener, creates a complex relationship compounded by the technologies involved in each step of the process. For the respondents, the shift from analog to digital has brought comparisons and tensions between changing technologies, processes, and practices with regard to approaches to recording and sound quality.

Digitization has transformed recording; wider access to once exclusively professional technology has revolutionized music making. Once the domain of the few, recording, arranging, and mixing on-screen through software such as Ableton and Pro Tools has brought music production to a mass audience. For those who have evolved in the recent affordable, domesticated, digital era this shift may be inconsequential—many producers began as hobbyists developing skills and practices using such software with no first-hand reference points from an analog past. For others who emerged at the onset of what was a costly digital upgrade, like producer Ben Edwards, this was initially prohibitive and substandard:

> *When I started out in the studio in the early 1990s digital audio was already well established. At the time I didn't fully embrace it, partly because not only was it much more expensive to buy into (in contrast to picking up what seemed like "discarded" analogue gear), but the 16-bit digital format also struck me as being sonically inferior.*

Other considerations with regard to changing working practices point to the convenience of limitless memory and recording options bringing offset by a seeming loss of recording intuition and decision-making:

> *As I have continued to work in the studio I have found another disadvantage working purely in the digital realm; with the ability to constantly recall music projects and songs I have found a tendency to put off committing to a final mix.*
>
> *(Ben Edwards—producer)*

This capacity update and perfect can result, as Edwards comments, in the temptation to:

> *[r]emove those imperfections and subtleties that breathe life into music and keep it interesting.*

The capability of digital technology to remove dirt or discoloration in the sound has meant producers seek to introduce analog tools and techniques into the process, to add a live feel to the process, observing that it can be:

> *[e]xhilarating to have a whole mix going on an analogue console, with its various associated external effect units and processors, knowing that the settings cannot be recalled later on. It makes you commit to a mix as if it were a live performance.*
>
> *(Ben Edwards—producer)*

This all implies a physicality to sound, which is fundamentally analog, and impacted by digitization. Imprinting sound waves to magnetic tape or to grooves on a record does not incur the same loss of information as their conversion to binary digital data. For some producers the tape itself embeds the dynamic characteristic of the sound; producer Joe Gastwirt believes that analog tape is "a much more musical medium … [its warmth acts like an instrument] and actually does something to the music" (Smith & McBride, 2005). However, this is texture that audio purists praise when they talk about "warmth," a reference to the slight amount of "distortion and compression built into" the analog tape (Gendron, 2005). For some digital natives, this may seem like an arcane process; for others, like music theorist Nick Katranis, the very physicality suggested by tape offers the capacity to capture something living, "the physical imprint of a sound wave, like a creature's body pressed into what becomes a fossil" (Reynolds, 2011, p. 313). However, collateral loss and conflict remain in these evolving technologies and changing practices.

How sound responds to changing technology and what is sacrificed in terms of perceptions of dynamic and "liveness" have created some concern for musicians. Broadband speeds, global access, and limitless choice have come at a cost for audio quality:

> *Digital, mostly compressed mp3, becomes harsh and physically tiring after listening for some time.*
>
> *(Respondent—producer)*

This apparent divergence where the digital technology offers much but often falls short would seem counterintuitive. As Sterne notes, "if we have possibilities for greater definition than before, why does so much audio appear to be moving in the opposite direction" (2012, p. 4). For some, this regression is a matter of compression for convenience, stating:

> *There is no inherent reason why digital music has to sound worse than analog; the problem was all in implementation and standards ... The mp3 is a digital compression technology that throws away a lot of information in order to reduce file size.*
>
> *Fukuyama (2011)*

> *Sound in the real world is analogue, even with the best forms of compression, and you are bound to lose elements of the original sound.*
>
> *(Respondent—producer)*

For some musicians, the convenience of online and mobile technology has impacted on the whole approach to music making and the craft of recording, suggesting that the listener's end-use has led to lowered expectations of sound quality:

> *There has been a slide downwards in sound recording, partly dictated by what we listen to music on mobile phones, iPods and through poor-quality headphones or small built-in speakers.*
>
> *(Phil Winter—musician)*

Although as another musician noted, history would suggest the technologies of listeners have always been of spectral and some of questionable quality:

> *We listened to shitty Decca record players, Tandy cassette players and medium wave radio in my analogue youth. Now we listen on laptops, iPods and phones, so no change really.*
>
> *(Steve Cobby—producer)*

5.8 Backward to the future

The shift to predominantly digital sound has been accompanied by a dramatic transformation in our understanding of music's function. This is not merely in technological terms but also the social, economic, and cultural conditions in which music and sound exist. How performance and live music are perceived in this new ecology is fundamental, with prerecorded sound and playback a common strategy for artists and DJs alike. The making and playing of music have manifestly been changed by digital technology, but importantly its shift to a compressed, binary form has meant its suitability for replication and easy movement through online technologies have impacted on how we perceive music and value it. The Internet has been addressed as a key agent of change, positioning the delivery system as the driver of new social and cultural practices. Music, no longer exclusively held in a tangible form, has been liberated into fluid and malleable information, which alongside still and moving images can be reshaped and moved on. Music has been decentered and displaced, but it remains dynamic and live in the broadest sense. It is important that we regard the Internet and mobile technologies not merely as a broadcast medium but also as a social, discursive medium.

We can no longer consider music making, live performance, and the music business as separate and distinct processes, but view them all in the context of "media forms" (Dubber, 2012, p. 14). Music, commodification, and commerce are inextricably linked but have required recalibration in the digital economy. These traditional parameters of music in the product age, if not mutually exclusive, have been considered autonomous processes constructed upon their economic activity. The erosion of these financial streams has left music and sound as active information to be repurposed and shared. This chapter, through responses of artists and producers, has attempted to articulate these changes. Clearly, the shift to digital has massively increased music's complexity and diversity, which in turn have been exacerbated by the productless nature of the online ecology. Regardless of exchange value, it is still all about the commodification of information, and the hyper-commodification of popular cultural forms (Sandywell & Beer, 2005, p. 107). This digital commodification has been progressed by the cut-and-paste, hybridization processes that characterize digital cultures. It is evident from the respondents and interviewees that perceptions of digital music forms still require reference to past analog traditions and practices. The loss of generic conventions does not entail the discarding of generic practices (Sandywell & Beer, 2005, p. 107). Artists, reluctant to dispose of established methods and protocols, instead are merely content to see them appropriated by digital technologies.

Though not always articulated, there was an inferred understanding that although considering themselves to be artists, respondents were fundamentally users accessing and repurposing sound. Attendant digital practices were not mutually exclusive, but common to all. The responses acknowledge the flexibility and accessibility of digital technologies in both recording and performance. Music, no longer fixed to a physical product, was now a discursive process driven by closer peer-to-peer relationships, with audiences and fellow artists engaging with, and exchanging, live and dynamic information.

References

Anderson, C. (2009). *Free: the future of a radical price*. London: Random House.

Bennett, L. (2012). Patterns of listening through social media: Online fan engagement with the live music experience. *Social Semiotics*, 22(5), 545–557.

Bruns, A. (2007). Beyond difference: Reconfiguring education for the user-led age. In *Proceedings ICE 3: Ideas, cyberspace, education, March 23, 2007*. Retrieved from http://eprints.qut.edu.au/6622.

Carr, N. (2008). *The big switch: Rewiring the world from Edison to Google*. New York: W.W. Norton & Co.

Chivers Yochim, E. & Biddinger, M. (2008). It kind of gives you that vintage feel: Vinyl records and the trope of death. *Media Culture Society*, 30(2), 183–195.

Derrida, J. (1994). *Spectres of Marx*. London: Routledge.

Dubber, A. (2012). *Music in the digital age*. Retrieved from https://leanpub.com/dubber.

Fukuyama, F. (2011). All hail … analog? *The Wall Street Journal*, Retrieved from http://online.wsj.com/article/SB10001424052748703529004576160300649048270.html.

Gendron, B. (2005). *Analog recording tries to survive a digital world.* Chicago Tribune. Retrieved from http://articles.chicagotribune.com/2005-01-16/news/0501160455_1_analog-recording-engineer-digital.

Kelly, K. (2002). *Where will music be coming from?* New York: New York Times Magazine. Retrieved from http://www.nytimes.com/2002/03/17/magazine/where-mu-sic-will-be-coming-from.html?pagewanted=all&src=pm.

Poster, M. (2004). Consumption and digital commodities in the everyday. *Cultural Studies*, 18(2–3), 409–423. Retrieved from http://dx.doi.org/10.1080/0950238042000201581.

Poster, M. (2005). Who controls digital culture? *Fast Capital*, 2(1). Retrieved from http://www.uta.edu/huma/agger/fastcapitalism/movie/poster.htm.

Reynolds, S. (2011). *Retromania: Popular culture's addiction to its own past.* London: Faber & Faber.

Sandywell, B. & Beer, D. (2005). Stylistic morphing: notes on the digitisation of contemporary music culture. *Convergence*, 11(4), 106–121.

Small, C. (1998). *Musicking: The meaning of performing and listening.* Middletown, CT: Wesleyan University Press.

Smith, E. & McBride, S. (2005). Tale of the tape. *Wall Street Journal*, Retrieved from http://permalink.gmane.org/gmane.comp.accessibility.vision/2518.

Sterne, J. (2012). *Mp3: The meaning of a format.* London: Duke University Press.

Toop, D. (2004). *Haunted weather.* London: Serpent's Tail.

Live from the ether: YouTube and live music video culture

6

A. Trainer

6.1 Introduction

There is little doubt that we have reached an age where information is in rampant surplus, and where concepts such as Web 2.0 and social networking are ingrained into the everyday. With these new frontiers of connectivity and accessibility now a vital part of our lived reality, there are few cultural repositories as vast or as pervasive as YouTube. Supplying a multitude of content, YouTube is a democratized virtual space where information is universally accessible, and where users are able to use increasingly straightforward means to share their own content. Without any tangible or corporeal form, this content comes seemingly from the ether—a space that is not only ethereal, but also quotidian—which surrounds us all.

It is the democracy and accessibility of both video recording technologies and YouTube as mediums for content sharing that has lead to the glut of live music content that can be found on the site. Although live music performances captured online may lack the directness and atmosphere of actually being there, as Auslander (2008) points out, "mediatized performance makes just as effective a focal point for the gathering of a social group as live performance" (p. 64) and online audiences find a number of ways in which to engage with and comment on live music.

From edited and produced content uploaded by artists, record labels, promoters, managers, and publicity personnel to raw, unedited and often poor-quality footage recorded on phones by fans, live music is a significant element of the YouTube experience. It facilitates a number of communities that are brought together virtually through an interest in live music, and often through a passion for archiving and sharing their musical tastes. Drawing on specific examples, and working through the Coachella Music festival as a case study, this chapter seeks to reconcile the numerous ways that artists and fans utilize YouTube as a site for music promotion, but also as a means of facilitating community.

6.2 Free-for-all: the YouTube model

YouTube exemplifies the "culture-sharing model" (Cheng, Dale, & Liu, 2007) that has developed online whereby individuals are able to upload and share their own content, as well as comment on the content of other users, and ultimately interact with one another and create communities based on their content and interests. As Manovich (2008) points out, we have witnessed "a gradual shift from the majority of Internet users accessing content produced by a much smaller number of professional

The Digital Evolution of Live Music

producers to users increasingly accessing content produced by other nonprofessional users" (p. 33). Similarly, artists and musicians are able to utilize these sites as promotional tools, creating their own channels with which to share content, and as an archival tool for promotional material, music videos, and recordings of live performances. Access to these sites is free, as is the capability to create and share content. The "constructs of gift and sharing economies describe the social contours of sites like YouTube, where users post content in order to share, without expectations of tangible compensation" (Lingel & Naaman, 2012, p. 335). It is for this reason that file sharing, and sites that rely on user-generated content, as well as content that operates around and in opposition to traditional notions of ownership and copyright, have become so popular. As exemplified by Kasaras (2002), the proliferation of file sharing and other new technologies that enable the free distribution of information, and in particular media such as music and video, has forced a radical recontextualization of the economic imperatives that drive the music industry. In an age where information is easily produced and shared, "the digital economy is one that has expanded so rapidly precisely because it has exploited the free labor of individual subjects" (Lingel & Naaman, 2012, p. 334). The propagation of user-created online content has been a significant part of this shifting cultural economy, not only away from the traditional model of paying for content but also in the capacity for users to create their own content, and to share content that may or may not be theirs to share. YouTube exemplifies this model.

The abundance of pirated or bootlegged material online has become increasingly concerning for copyright holders. Despite the efforts of publishers and copyright holders to restrict their material from being pirated, in many instances, such as on YouTube, there is no way to stop individuals from uploading and sharing copyright-restricted content. And while the capacity may exist for copyright holders to take action to remove their intellectual property from YouTube, the reality is that it may be reposted elsewhere as soon as it is removed, with the prospect of this occurring so likely that many copyright holders choose not to act. Nolin refers to YouTube as a "copygrey service" (2010, p. 16). As a host of user-uploaded content, YouTube presents itself as a legitimately democratized platform that serves as an intermediary between content and audience. However, it is the user's interpretation of this service, and their relationship with (and at times disregard for) copyright that blurs the lines of legitimacy. Further complicating this relationship is the use of YouTube for the uploading of content that may use copyrighted material for its own purposes, such as the "parody videos" discussed by Erickson, Mendis, and Kretschmer (2013) that reframe original content in contexts that are either personalized or directed toward specific communities. YouTube has been accused of operating under the illusion of being a "[u]topian experiment" (Blakely, 2006, p. 38) while using a strategically implemented business model to generate considerable profits through advertising. The implication for the individual of this supposed utopianism is the ability to create their own experience of the site, by selecting only content that has relevance to their interests and by uploading content that they value and wish to share with others. In the instance of live music fans, YouTube offers the opportunity for individuals to create and engage with content that hails their specific experience or interest, and to operate as part of a community that is dedicated to that interest.

6.3 It's all here: community and access

The concept of community has shifted significantly in the digital age, and specifically as a result of Web 2.0 technology. While communities based around specific cultural cues or texts previously grew from social interactivity mostly based around shared space, and were generally geographically contextualized, this has changed significantly. Rotman et al. comment that although "YouTube is not often considered an online community, the rich user-generated content and personal communication tools that are offered to YouTube users may aid in creating a cohesive users' community" (2009, p. 41). This community is generated around shared cultural experience but is completely removed from the geographical or locational contexts that have framed traditional thinking around community dynamics. Donath (2007) refers to social network sites as inherently egocentric in the sense that our navigation of them is fundamentally limited to and restricted by our individual tastes, habits, and personal predilections. Similarly, these sites "allow for the public display of interpersonal commentary" (p. 232), which facilitates the development and interaction of online communities, and also allows for the individual to negotiate these communities and the content through which they are mapped. Because the online world operates outside of traditional geographical space, the appreciation of and engagement with live music culture online recontextualizes the discursive structures of live music as it pertains to space and place. While the experience of a live performance was previously restricted to physical attendance of that performance, the uploading of live material extends the ability to experience a live performance, albeit in a significantly augmented and ultimately reduced capacity, to anyone in any location globally.

The proliferation of both user-generated and user-captured content on YouTube has changed the economy of information, which has significant implications for recorded footage of live musical performances. Previously, the only way to witness live performances by a specific artist after the fact was through officially released label-sanctioned consumer-oriented materials such as live DVDs, video-cassettes, and even theatrically released concert films, or concert footage appearing on television. With YouTube acting as a repository for much of this content, official streaming video content of live performances is more prolific and accessible than was previously possible. This footage is professionally shot, edited, and commercially released, and it presents the artists and their image as commercially managed and marketed. However, in many instances this material, while originating as officially approved and artist-sanctioned, makes its way onto YouTube via fans who record, document, and upload it without the permission of the artist, their management, or the original content owner. Again, Nolin's notion of "copygrey" material is summoned (2010), and in many instances this material goes unchecked or unimpinged by copyright law. Many users choose to offer disclaimers in the descriptions of their videos claiming no ownership or copyright to the content they have uploaded. Hilderbrand (2007) comments that "YouTube has become one of the most prominent and popular sites where what's actually legal law is being contested and potentially curtailed" (p. 56), and while much of what is posted on YouTube is either subject to copyright or contains appropriated content, the site survives arguably due to the proportional amount of material that in no way infringes copyright. The distinctions between artist-sanctioned YouTube content and user-uploaded copied content are subtle, but present on YouTube. While many users are unconcerned with the source of the material that they search for, the benefit to artists and labels of controlling their official content is the same as controlling any officially marketed and promoted communication.

6.4 Another promotional tool: the official model

Because YouTube operates via channels, content featuring or tagging a particular artist may be accessible from a range of channels, including the band's own official channel, that of their record label, or numerous fan channels. For example, a search for "Madonna" returns a number of items that are hosted on various channels, including live content, content from television, music videos, and fan-created content that uses Madonna's music. This content is hosted across a number of official channels, including "The Official Madonna YouTube Channel," "Warner Bros. Records," and "GLAAD"—which features a video of Madonna presenting the Vito Russell award to journalist Anderson Cooper at the GLAAD Media Awards (GLAAD, 2013). However, the bulk of the material hosted on official channels is promotional in nature and is represented mostly by music videos. The majority of live content is hosted elsewhere, on channels that appear to be both artist-sanctioned but unrelated to the artist or her label, such as the LoveLiveTV channel, which features a video entitled "Madonna Live At Paris Olympia 2012 OFFICIAL HD Director's Cut Full Show," and user-created unofficial channels. However, Madonna's own official YouTube channel does feature archival material of early live performances, such as an early live performance of the song "Everybody" at the Danceteria night club in New York from December 1982 (Madonna, 2013a). Other live performance videos on Madonna's official channel include a 50-second video shot on either portable digital camera or phone camera, which captures a brief exchange between Madonna and a fan (Madonna, 2013b), and many other excerpts from shows—not necessarily capturing live performances, but behind-the-scenes footage and notable excerpts or momentary vignettes from soundchecks and tour dates. Several of these videos also feature the moments during Madonna performances where she speaks about human rights and freedom of speech and identity.

Madonna's official YouTube live performance content exemplifies the ways in which an artist's public image can be managed by utilizing specific content to highlight particular elements of their career, or issues that are relevant to their public image. Through live performance content this is done seemingly casually, as much of the live content appears to be randomly captured moments shot handheld in low resolution that have not been professionally edited. YouTube's immediacy and low cost enable artists to present what may appear to be casual and candid moments that characterize them in a specific way, and which enable them to project a particular image, or to highlight certain facets of their creative persona.

Throughout her career, Madonna has had a strong following in the queer community, with both gay and lesbian fans engaging with her music and imagery (Schwichtenberg, 1992). In 2012 she faced accusations from the Russian government of promoting homosexual behavior at a concert in St. Petersburg (Vinter, 2012), and was also openly critical of the Russian government's treatment of jailed performance artists Pussy Riot. As of early 2013, specific instances of the live content on the official Madonna YouTube channel were directly linked to her standing in the queer community, and arguably aimed at addressing the charges against her by the Russian government. A specific video entitled "Madonna's Full St. Petersburg Speech" (Madonna, 2013c) captures the event in question, and was uploaded days after the concert took place. This video has a number of functions. It operates as a statement by the artist in regards to the accusations, but it also acts as a promotional product, presenting the kind of inclusive atmosphere and political platform that is promoted at a Madonna concert. This live performance video serves as a further promotional tool for Madonna within the queer community, and in a more general sense as an ambassador of a particular politics of inclusion. The potential for artists to use the live arena as a means of political debate has always existed, but YouTube now allows for those messages to reach larger audiences, and to operate as a means for a specific kind of promotion for that artist.

Given the economic transition that has taken place in the music industry away from album sales and toward live performance (Mortimer, Nosko, & Sorensen, 2012), the uploading of live material to an artist's YouTube channel can be perceived as an opportunity not only to promote that artist's brand and music but also to publicly shape perceptions about the live performance aspect of their career. By tailoring specific moments from live shows that are distributed to their fans via the artist's official channel, YouTube enables performers to manage the expectations of their fans with regards to their live show, to provide an example of what to expect from their live show. It is arguably for this reason that artists and labels may choose not to remove unofficially uploaded live footage from other users. Despite a breach of copyright, and the potential loss of income from sales, or the devaluing of brand through this copyright infringed sharing, there is value to the artists of their performance being available publicly. As Mortimer et al. (2012) point out, the availability of music through file sharing has had an inverse effect on record sales and the number of live performances taking place, with the former dropping and the latter increasing. Similarly, the possibility for the availability of a specific performance on YouTube to incite further ticket sales is particularly viable, as is the possibility of exposure to that content having a positive effect on an artist's popularity through related activity around or because of it.

Often the only live performance material that appears on a well-known artist's official YouTube channel will be live performances recorded for television. For example, both Foo Fighters and TV On the Radio feature video footage of their performances on The Late Show with David Letterman. These videos are shot in a professional context, and they offer a rare or exclusive opportunity to view an artist performing new material live, as these performances are usually recorded to coincide with a new album release. Although this may change if an artist records a tour video or uploads content shot while performing live (such as Madonna's live excerpts), live performance material is usually only a single track in length. Officially shot, full concert footage is most readily posted onto YouTube by users who have no copyright claims to the content. However, as Hilderbrand points out, YouTube remains online due to "the indisputable volume of material that in no way infringes copyright and that can be argued to reflect the experiences and ideas of a generation and possibly even a whole cultural moment" (2007, p. 56). While YouTube offers material that in many instances infringes copyright, much like peer-to-peer file sharing, the sheer volume of material shared and the remaining availability of the technology responsible for video sharing ensure that removing said content is largely futile.

6.5 Identifying the fanvid: the amateur–professional divide

For less established artists, the potential exists for officially sanctioned live footage, albeit lacking in either video or audio quality (and often both), to offer a promotional opportunity that due to the prohibitive cost of professionally recording either live performances or other promotional content such as music videos offers stop-gap promotional content. McLeod (2005) makes the point with regards to file sharing that can be applied equally to YouTube that these technologies offer "the potential to create an alternative means of music distribution for artists who are often marginalized by the mainstream music industry" (p. 521). Exemplifying this model are a series of eight videos uploaded to YouTube by Dylan Baillie in April 2013, of Winnipeg post-hardcore outfit KEN Mode performing songs from their album "Entrench" at the live show promoting the album's release (KEN-mode, 2013). While the multicamera approach used for this series of videos offers clear, crisp, archive-friendly images, the audio recording of these videos on the other hand is arguably lifted from in-camera microphones, and is resultingly muffled. However, the band chose to promote these videos on their website, offering them as documentation of their live sound and performance style, and using them as a promotional tool, and as a way of engaging with their audience—such as through the possibility for YouTube users to comment on videos—in order to reach them directly. Hilderbrand points out that "[a]s documents, the low-resolution postings to YouTube fall far short of archival preservation" (2007, p. 54), but for many grassroots performers, the benefits of promoting their music outweigh the necessity to use less-than-perfect audio or video.

Varying video and audio quality are symptomatic of much live material uploaded to YouTube. Often the audio quality of live recordings uploaded to YouTube is muddy and lacking in clarity or dynamic. The video accompanying it is often single-camera, handheld and therefore shaky or overly static and immobile, suggesting that the camera operator may have left the camera set up in a single position for the entirety of the performance. Additionally, these images can tend to be out of focus, have poor color balance, and contain digital noise or pixilation due to poor light conditions. However, the implications for nonprofessional musicians to have their music available to potential audiences regardless of the aesthetic pitfalls of its production arguably make the decision to upload imperfect video worthwhile. This plays into a number of assumptions about the merits and worth of art, regardless of its aesthetics or the manner in which it is presented to the public. Benjamin (1968) and Baudrillard (1994) were both concerned with the supposed loss of value that exists as the result of reproduction, and

Cayari (2011) has adapted this concern with reference to YouTube and its reproduction of live or second-hand events through digital means. Tirrell also points out that aesthetic degradation "only makes sense if one imposes a hierarchy in which an arbitrary original functions as the archetype to which other objects are expected to conform" (2010, p. 148). YouTube arguably recontextualizes that hierarchy through its function as a repository for simulacra—an archive of material recorded from second- or third-hand sources, or of material recorded in nonprofessional or amateur situations.

It can often be difficult to ascertain whether the amateur live footage uploaded to YouTube of less popular or lesser-known musicians is artist-sanctioned or not, whether it has been uploaded by the band or a user associated with the band, or whether this content falls into the category of fan videos. It is even more difficult to ascertain when the audio or video quality of the videos is lacking. While any artist can create their own YouTube channel, often grassroots performers leave this to others, and live music content is often uploaded by individuals under usernames or avatars. As Sherman (2008) points out, video is no longer "the exclusive medium of technicians or specialists or journalists or artists—it is the people's medium" (p. 161). As an example, a series of videos uploaded by user Kennysmith in 2008 of a then recent performance of Melbourne band Eddy Current Suppression Ring at the Excelsior Hotel in Sydney (Kennysmith, 2013) feature many of the characteristics of amateur fan videos—static camera, blurred focus, and muddy sound. Given the DIY aesthetic with which Eddy Current Suppression Ring is readily identified subculturally, it is possible that these videos were sanctioned by the band, but it is more likely that they belong to the category of fan videos—content uploaded by users and not associated with the band in any way. With regard to the aesthetic imperfections and relative lack of professional presentation of much of this YouTube content, Richard (2008) asks, "are they the products of 'media amateurs' or do we have to find new specifications and descriptions for the producers" (p. 142). This is arguably the type of situation that requires a new definition for those creating media texts. Through advancements in personal technologies such as digital video cameras and camera phones, it is now possible for anyone with access to these technologies to upload their own live recording of an artist to YouTube, and for fans to access multiple recordings of a particular artist, and even multiple recordings of the same performance. Bird (2011) offers the term "produsers" as a description of contemporary subjects whose relationship with the media encompasses both consumption or use, and active engagement and production. While a clear division previously existed between those creating media and those consuming it, Web 2.0 technology—including platforms such as YouTube—has offered a democratization that has forced us to recontextualize not only how texts are created and shared but why.

6.6 The heart of copygrey: the user-generated model

YouTube actualizes Richard's assertion of the need for a new set of definitions for media creation (2008). Why then do amateur filmmakers and fans upload these blurry, pixilated videos with muddy, imperfect sound to YouTube? Waldron (2013) asserts that YouTube videos "act as vehicles of agency to promote and engage participatory culture through discourse in online community" (p. 94). For artists who may not have the means to produce professional video documentation or promotional material, the choice to have some outlet for their art is a simple one to make. However, for fans or other users the reasoning becomes more complex. As Lingel & Naaman (2012) point out, there is no tangible incentive for YouTube users to share their content, but the nontangible incentives are multiple. Cover (2006) suggests that online environments such as YouTube offer the opportunity for users to recontextualize the relationship between authors, texts, and audiences in order to attain a participatory sense of authorship. Donath (2007) points to identity formation as a primary motivation for YouTube users, while Huberman et al. (2009) detail the impetus behind information sharing through communal crowdsourcing as attention, with value being placed on viewership statistics, comments from other users, and "favoriting" by other users.

In this way, YouTube offers individuals the opportunity to recontextualize the creation of content by presenting content that they may have had little to no input into the creation of, and which may fall into the category of nonprofessional fan video, for example, the posting of amateur concert videos of established music acts by fans. Suffering from many of the aesthetic downfalls as much amateur YouTube content—such as pixilated or grainy video, muffled audio, and unsteady handheld camerawork—many of these videos nonetheless receive thousands of views, are favorited by other users, and receive numerous comments, most of which are generally positive. In this way they can be seen to be accomplishing the nontangible incentives for posting content, and fulfilling the user's motivation for doing so.

As Lange (2007) points out, the comments' section of YouTube is often rife with trolling and other forms of antagonism based on the anonymity of posting on a virtual forum. However, when the content of a video is more specialized, such as a live performance from a specific artist, the discussion is more likely to focus on the content of the video, the artists and their creative legacy or back-catalog, and discussion of other performances by that artist. This is often dependent on the artist, as there are certain types of content that tend to either provoke trolling or attract users who are more likely to engage in trolling or antagonistic posting. For example, user The Veepas posted 11 videos from 2 different concerts by Canadian progressive rock band Rush filmed in Pittsburgh from 2010 to 2012 (The Veepas, 2013). These videos received between 300 and 10,000 views each over the course of two years and six months online, respectively. All of the comments posted by other users on these videos were focused on Rush's music, including significant praise for the band musically, and discussions of the differences between specific performances and tours. Many of those who comment on these videos arguably feel a deep engagement with the music, regardless of inferior visual or audio quality of the video on which it features, and the motivation for their comments would appear to be the community that Rotman, Golbeck, and Preece (2009) discuss in their analysis of YouTube users. For the user who uploads these videos, however, there appears to be a motivation to archive an experience that has personal significance, but which may otherwise be lost to time and memory. As Pietrobruno (2013) points out, YouTube as a medium allows for the "social archiving of intangible heritage" (p. 2) in allowing those aspects of our everyday experience—which might otherwise be lost to the ether—to live on. Cha et al. (2007) discuss the notion of personal archiving as a strong impetus behind an activity that holds no tangible incentives. The desire to capture, catalog, and make available the minutiae of one's life to whomever is interested taps into the notion of the very human desire of wanting to leave an imprint and to leave something of value either for ourselves or for one another, either those we know or complete strangers (Wesch, 2009). Many YouTube channels exemplify this approach to the phenomenon, offering personalized archives of live performances by artists with whom the user has an affinity or connection.

6.7 Offsetting copygrey: YouTube services

Although YouTube is unable to monitor the content uploaded by all of its many millions of users, it has taken steps in recent years to divert attention away from the various types of usage of the site and its status as a copygrey service, toward a position embracing its potential for live interaction. In July 2009, a new channel emerged on YouTube entitled YouTube Presents, which was described on the channel itself as showcasing "live music and exclusive performances" from a variety of artists representing a number of genres and musical communities (YouTube Presents, 2013). All of these performances were filmed in a studio in front of small audiences and were promoted as intimate opportunities to showcase the music of a particular artist. These performances were streamed live on YouTube and were advertised on the website in advance. Some of the performances remain on the channel in their entirety while others have been removed and remain only as short clips.

Live streaming on YouTube began in 2009 (Parr, 2009), with one-off events such as live music concerts, sporting matches, and political interviews being broadcast and available on the website after streaming. Live streaming on the site from this point was occasional but consistent. In April 2011, the site launched a new initiative named YouTube Live, which integrated live streaming capabilities and other tools directly into the YouTube platform (YouTube Live, 2013). After the introduction of YouTube Live, a number of channels were introduced dedicated to live music, sports, news, and gaming. The live music channel streams content from a range of broadcasters including record labels, radio stations, artists, even schools, and other grassroots organizations that wish to create live streams of their events.

The implications for YouTube's live streaming facility are similar to the way in which users engage with the site generally. While the vast majority of content created and broadcast on the site will appeal to only a niche audience, and may only ever be accessed by those directly involved in the content, there also exists the potential for simultaneous live streaming by significant communities of users globally. Exemplifying the former are live events by schools, religious groups, and other community organizations, such as the Phoenix Christian School PreK-8 Spring Concert, which streamed live on YouTube on April 26, 2013, and was streamed live by 31 viewers on the school's YouTube channel (PHXCRC, 2013). Dozens of similar events take place across YouTube channels on a weekly basis. By offering the ability to publicly live-stream events such as these, YouTube offers grassroots organizations the opportunity to further engage with and potentially foster and build connections within their communities, as well as effectively to document and later archive their events. However, the implications for larger events with a greater potential viewership to reach significant numbers offers a recontexualization of the ways in which we think about live music.

6.8 A live-streaming case study: Coachella

The Coachella Valley Music and Arts Festival has been held in the Californian city of Indio since 1999 (Robison, 2008), beginning as a two-day festival and expanding to a three-day festival held over two weekends in 2013, with a daily attendance of over 80,000 (Firecloud, 2013). The festival focuses on music performances by a range of artists, including globally established and recognized performers, as well as younger emerging artists performing across genres such as pop music, indie rock, and various genres or styles of dance and electronic music. The festival has also, due largely to the acts appearing on the line-up, and the popularity of outdoor festivals with a particular demographic, gained a reputation for attracting an audience characterized as being mostly in their early-twenties to early-thirties, generally middle-class to affluent, and well connected through social media and other forms of online communication. Since 2010 the festival has also set up a live stream on YouTube, with performances from the festival's main stages being broadcast live, and restreamed during the hours outside of festival performances. It is important to note that within the specific subcultural or demographic demarcation to which the Coachella festival is marketed, online culture is a significant tool for absorbing and engaging with other facets of culture such as music and fashion. Coachella's (2013) live YouTube stream was reported on and marketed across a number of blogs and websites oriented around popular culture and music, and was marketed as an online event.

In 2013, the festival streamed live on Coachella's YouTube channel across both weekends that it ran—April 12–14 and 19–21. Three stages were available to stream simultaneously and viewers were able to scroll between all three, and to leave messages, similar to a twitter feed. The creation of a live stream of the festival on YouTube is an important factor in reaching a demographic that is characterized as living increasingly online, and as being overly concerned with contemporary notions of fashion, authenticity, and popular cultural capital. During the festival's first weekend, Coachella's live stream on YouTube reached over 5 million views, with thousands of simultaneous views occurring throughout the event (Coachella, 2013). Whilst the majority of YouTube interaction with Coachella appeared on the festival's own channel, a number of broadcasts from unofficial sources emerged only hours after the original content had aired. For example, headline act Blur's set was broadcast live but not restreamed on the Coachella channel. Broadcasts of the performance began to emerge a day after it originally aired live on Coachella's channel, first with single tracks from the performance and then with several full versions of the set.

A version of the band's performance of their song "Tender" emerged a day after it first aired, uploaded by user happygabri, receiving over 300 plays within one day, over 2,000 within two weeks, and over 8,000 within a month (2013). Two full versions of the performance emerged shortly afterward, featuring varying visual and audio quality. Two weeks after being uploaded, the lower-quality version had received over 29,000 views, and the higher-quality version had received over 66,000 views. These figures indicate that a higher-quality version of a live performance will be likely to receive more views, but this is not always the case. A low-quality version of Tame Impala's Coachella (2013) set uploaded by user Pablo Contreras received over 47,000 plays during the two weeks after it was first uploaded (2013), whereas a higher-quality version uploaded by user efevelasquez had received just under 11,000 views over the same period (2013). Although it is possible that this video's significantly lower viewership statistics may be attributed to having being posted two days after Pablo Contrera's, a more likely reason may be the fact that efevelasquez had only 42 subscribers to his channel, on which he had uploaded only four videos. Comparatively, Pablo Contrera had 431 subscribers for 13 videos. Although the majority of videos uploaded by each user were from Coachella (2013), Pablo Contrera had been a member since 2006, while efevelasquez had only been a member since 2010. All these elements factor into the popularity and use of specific content on YouTube. While it is often difficult to ascertain specific statistical information for many YouTube videos as many users tend to disable the public viewing of statistical information from their accounts, framing specific content in this way offers further clarification on the ways in which live music-based YouTube content is accessed and the ways in which viewers engage with it.

Coachella's live-streaming exemplifies the potential for YouTube to connect with existing music audiences and for those audiences to engage with relevant content simultaneously. Live-streaming music events transcend their geographical location by connecting audiences that are scattered globally, but who share a similar passion or interest. In addition, the audio feed for live-streaming often comes as a live, direct feed from the mixing console, and is often therefore superior to the live sound that is being projected to thousands of concertgoers via live amplification, and may be affected by position in the crowd or by wind disturbances. Similarly, the multicamera feed of an event such as Coachella, with close-ups of solos and other imaginative editing, arguably ensures that those watching a live stream will often be able to observe more of the detail of a performance than those who may attend it but who are located away from the stage. For the fans who may not be able to travel to an event, live-streaming offers a consolation, if not a comparable experience. Although the experience of physically attending a live music event cannot be replicated, live-streaming does provide a real-time engagement with events as they unfold, which although no physically different from experiencing an upload after the event, still holds a significant benefit for the viewer by operating in real time so that they are able to experience a performance as it unfolds, alongside with those who are actually there, albeit virtually. The implications of live-streaming on YouTube for online communities are multitudinous, but its ability to bring together specific audiences through live music is continually proven through events such as Coachella.

6.9 Conclusion

As Bennett (2012) points out with reference to virtual interaction with live music events, "[d]istinctions between being there and participating remotely may become further blurred and continue to be re-negotiated as technology develops, but this will also confirm that 'being there,' whatever that means, is the musical experience fans most value" (p. 555). Whilst video footage of live music performances and live-streaming of music events can never hope to match, let alone surpass, the experience of attending a live music event, these mediums offer a number of ways in which online subjects are able to engage with and participate in making of meaning from live music.

The implications for live music content on sites such as YouTube are myriad. In thinking about YouTube as a social website built around the uploading, viewing, and sharing of content, the potential exists for a new era of live bootlegging, with users able to upload and share self-recorded material of live music performances. Conversely, official label- or artist-sanctioned or operated YouTube channels offer the opportunity for video footage of live performances to become part of the marketing and audience engagement strategies for artists at any level of their career. The implications for those looking to engage with live music content as consumers are also multitudinous.

Although nebulous, the communities formed online around live music on platforms such as YouTube create their own rules of engagement, and offer rewards to those who wish to participate in the sharing and discussion of live music culture online. Through their constancy and potential to permanently update and replenish the information they provide, YouTube offers users an experience that allows them to create their own methods of engagement with texts, artists, and live music experiences, and to renegotiate the ways in which they think about and participate in live music culture.

References

Auslander, P. (2008). *Liveness: Performance in a mediatized culture*. Oxon: Routledge.

Baudrillard, J. (1994). *Simulacra and simulation*. Ann Arbor: University of Michigan Press.

Benjamin, W. (1937/1968). The work of art in the age of mechanical reproduction. H. Zohn, Trans. In Arendt, H. (Ed.), *Illuminations: essays and reflections*. New York: Schocken.

Bennett, L. (2012). Patterns of listening through social media: online fan engagement with the live music experience. *Social Semiotics*, 22(5), 545–557.

Bird, S. E. (2011). Are we all producers now? Convergence and media audience practices. *Cultural Studies*, 25(4–5), 502–516.

Blakely, R. (2006). *YouTube copyright*: Final 2 Edition. London: The Times. October 28, 36.

Cayari, C. (2011). The YouTube effect: How YouTube has provided new ways to consume, create, and share music. *International Journal of Education and the Arts*, 12(6), 1–28. Retrieved from http://www.ijea.org/v12n6.

Cha, M., Kwak, H., Rodriguez, P., Ahn, Y. Y., & Moon, S. (2007). I tube, you tube, everybody tubes: analyzing the world's largest user generated content video system. In *Proceedings of the 7th ACM SIGCOMM conference on Internet measurement*, 1–14.

Cheng, X., Dale, C., & Liu, J. (2007). *Understanding the characteristics of internet short video sharing: YouTube as a case study*. Retrieved from http://arxiv.org/abs/0707.3670.

Coachella. (2013). *Coachella YouTube profile*. Retrieved from http://www.youtube.com/user/coachella.

Contreras, P. (2013). *Tame Impala—Live@Coachella festival (full performance)*. Retrieved from http://www.youtube.com/watch?v=_XDJazhT-B4.

Cover, R. (2006). Audience inter/active: Interactive media, narrative control and reconceiving audience history. *New Media & Society*, 8(1), 139–158.

Donath, J. (2007). Signals in social supernets. *Journal of Computer-Mediated Communication*, 13(1), 231–251.

efevelasquez (2013). *Tame Impala@Coachella 2013 [COMPLETE HD SHOW]*Retrieved from http://www.youtube.com/watch?v=4-LQvIKA8AI.

Erickson, K., Mendis, D., & Kretschmer, M. (2013). *Copyright and the economic effects of parody: An empirical study of music videos on the YouTube platform and an assessment of the regulatory options*. Project Report, London: Intellectual Property Office, pp. 1–34.

Firecloud, J. (2013). *Coachella by the numbers: The attendance explosion continues*. Crave. Retrieved from http://www.craveonline.com/music/articles/477705-coachella-by-the-numbers-the-attendance-explosion-continuess.

GLAAD (2013). *Madonna presents the Vito Russell Award to Anderson Cooper at #glaad-award*. Retrieved from http://www.youtube.com/watch?v=ZI7wRDMsk5k.

Happygabri (2013). *Blur—Tender LIVE @ COACHELLA*. Retrieved from http://www.youtube.com/watch?v=K_CLQ9cQaoU.

Hilderbrand, L. (2007). YouTube: Where cultural memory and copyright converge. *Film Quarterly*, 61(1), 48–57.

Huberman, B. A., Romero, D. M., & Wu, F. (2009). Crowdsourcing, attention and productivity. *Journal of Information Science*, 35(6), 758–765.

Kasaras, K. (2002). Music in the age of free distribution—Mp3 and society. *First Monday*, 7(1). Retrieved from http://firstmonday.org/htbin/cgiwrap/bin/ojs/index.php/fm/article/viewArticle/927/8.

KEN-Mode.com (2013). Retrieved from http://www.ken-mode.com.

Kennysmith (2013). *Kennysmith's YouTube channel*. Retrieved from http://www.youtube.com/user/Kennysmith?feature.

Lange, P. G. (2007). Commenting on comments: Investigating responses to antagonism on YouTube. In *Annual Conference of the Society for Applied Anthropology* (p. 29).

Lingel, J., & Naaman, M. (2012). You should have been there, man: Live music, DIY content and online communities. *New Media Society*, 14(2), 332–349.

Madonna (2013a). *Madonna—live at the Danceteria*. Retrieved from http://www.youtube.com/watch?v=ttJBJTcnroc.

Madonna (2013b). *True blue for like a prayer in Vancouver—September 30*. Retrieved from http://www.youtube.com/watch?v=0Q2yR58wNH8&list=UU81VD6eeuLLSfyY_D-N8s-Vw&index=6.

Madonna (2013c) *Madonna's full St. Petersburg speech*. Retrieved from http://www.youtube.com/user/madonna?feature=watch (accessed April 5, 2013).

Manovich, L. (2008). The practice of everyday (media) life. In G. Lovink & S. Niederer (Eds), *Video vortex reader: Responses to YouTube* (pp. 33–44). Amsterdam: Institute of Network Cultures.

McLeod, K. (2005). MP3s are killing home taping: The rise of internet distribution and its challenge to the major label music monopoly. *Popular Music and Society*, 28(4), 521–531.

Mortimer, J. H., Nosko, C., & Sorensen, A. (2012). Supply responses to digital distribution: Recorded music and live performances. *Information Economics and Policy*, 24(1), 3–14.

Parr, B. (2009). *YouTube to live stream U2 concert*. Mashable. Retrieved from http://mashable.com/2009/10/19/u2-youtube-live-stream.

PHXCRC (2013). *PHXCRC YouTube profile*. Retrieved from http://www.youtube.com/user/PHXCRC.

Pietrobruno, S. (2013). YouTube and the social archiving of intangible heritage. *New Media & Society*, 15(8), 1259–1276. Retrieved from http://nms.sagepub.com/content/early/2013/01/08/1461444812469598.

Richard, B. (2008). Media masters and grassroot art 2.0 on YouTube. In G. Lovink & S. Niederer (Eds), *Video vortex reader: Responses to YouTube* (pp. 141–152). Amsterdam: Institute of Network Cultures.

Robison, G. (2008). *Coachella*. New York: Rosen Central.

Rotman, D., Golbeck, J., & Preece, J. (2009). The community is where the rapport is—on sense and structure in the Youtube community. In *Proceedings of the fourth international conference on communities and technologies, ACM*. 41–50.

Schwichtenberg, C. (1992). Madonna's postmodern feminism: Bringing the margins to the center. *Southern Journal of Communication*, 57(2), 120–131.

Sherman, T. (2008). Vernacular video. In G. Lovink & S. Niederer (Eds), *Video vortex reader: Responses to YouTube* (pp. 161–168). Amsterdam: Institute of Network Cultures.

The Veepas (2013). *The Veepas YouTube profile*. Retrieved from http://www.youtube.com/user/TheVeepas/videos.

Vinter, P. (2012). *Madonna faces legal action after Russian activists claim she encouraged gay sex between children during show in St. Petersburg*. Daily Mail. Retrieved from http://www.dailymail.co.uk/news/article-2219128/Madonna-appears-Russian-court-face-accusations-encouraged-gay-sex-minors.html.

Waldron, J. (2013). YouTube, fanvids, forums, vlogs and blogs: Informal music learning in a convergent on-and offline music community. *International Journal of Music Education*, 31(1), 91–105.

Wesch, M. (2009). The machine is (changing) us: YouTube culture and the politics of authenticity. In *Personal democracy forum*. Retrieved from http://www.YouTube.com/watch?v=09gR6VPVrpw.

YouTube Live (2013). *YouTube live*. Retrieved from http://www.youtube.com/live/all.

YouTube Presents (2013). *YouTube presents*. Retrieved from http://www.youtube.com/user/YouTubePresents.

Live music in a virtual world: exuberant flourishing and disability at Wheelies nightclub in Second Life

7

M. Kent, K. Ellis

Virtual world nightclub founder Simon Stevens has described the dance floor of the once-popular Second Life venue Wheelies as a unique example of how people with disabilities and the "nondisabled" can come together for enjoyment and celebration (2011). An award-winning disability issues consultant and person with cerebral palsy, Stevens established the online club in 2006, the same year he became the first Second Life resident to have his avatar use a wheelchair in the Linden Lab online world. The nightclub has catered both to people with disabilities and those who do not present as such. Although previous and current managers position the club as disability themed rather than a disabled club, Wheelies has been described as a pioneering example of disability inclusion through virtual community, particularly in light of its "sign language displays and wheelchair-friendly dances" (Smith, 2012). The club won the Catalyst Award in the United Kingdom in the revolutionary category in 2008, for outstanding use of social media and technology that leads to social change.

Live music is integral to Wheelies' success story and its impact on disability social change online. As Hickey-Moody and Wood (2010) suggest, "the attraction to Wheelies is the music, live artists, dance and contests. Also a safe place to have fun with no pressure to disclose anything about one's abilities or disabilities in real life." In a personal interview for this book chapter, Stevens (2013) agrees live music is an attractive feature: "There is nothing like live music, in terms of hearing the DJ or artist speak to and interacting with the avatars in the club, and to be able to request music." The issue of disability disclosure is central to arguments regarding people with disabilities' use of social media for social change. As a disability-themed nightclub, Wheelies promotes an inclusive environment through the streaming of live music. It offers a place for people to express their disability pride through their avatars and through that a political message of inclusion and acceptance.

Beers and Geesin (2009) have cautioned that music and performance in Second Life should not be seen as directly analogous with its analog counterparts. Ultimately behind each avatar in Second Life, there is a person sitting alone at a computer screen; he/she may be in a room with other people present, but his/her attention is directed at the screen, and through the screen in the digital virtual world, live music can be performed and appreciated by a live digital audience embodied through a variety of Second Life avatars that cohabit the same shared virtual space. When Wheelies is inactive, a Second Life radio channel plays to an empty room; without the live interaction it is just a space in Second Life with good lighting. However, add the virtual projection

The Digital Evolution of Live Music

of a live DJ or performer, avatars dancing, and a crowd to appreciate the performance, and the virtual space becomes real and alive. Everyone, both performers and audience, is in the analog world alone with their computers, but at that same time they are in a shared virtual space singing, dancing, and having an authentic experience of live music. Kazoo Twang, a Second Life performer, says of performing in the virtual world, "I think we do something rather more special than singing to a karaoke machine. It may not be perfect but it is most definitely LIVE!!!!" (Voodoo, 2008). These virtual spaces may lack the smell of sweat and drinks that a person might experience at an analog concert, but they do have their own unique shared space, and through Wheelies, unlike at many analog performances, people with disabilities are included and represented.

During 2006, when the entrepreneurial virtual world Second Life achieved "mainstream status" (Smith, 2012), much was said about its potential to include and empower people with disabilities. For example, initial reports focused on the ways people with disabilities could hide their disabled embodiment by electing to have able-bodied avatars:

> *[Niles Sopor] has found an opportunity to forget his disability and experience walking life through his avatar. "Perhaps the most profound difference I have experienced is that people have treated me differently," he said. "In real life, due to my wheelchair and lack of physical coordination, people often regard me as intellectually as well as physically disabled."*
>
> *Cassidy (2007)*

> *Part of the pleasure in using SL is being able to transcend ... disability and interact "normally." I want to get away from the need for wheelchair accessible entrances, ramps, curb cuts, guide dogs, and all the other things we associate with physical limitations.*
> *After all, in SL I can fly. Why would I want to create another world in which I can't even get around without special accommodation?*
>
> *"Eli," quoted in Friedkin (2008)*

This echoes much early rhetoric of the liberatory potential of the Internet when it was widely considered much of people's attraction to communicating in online worlds lay in their ability to both hide and fabricate aspects of identity. Niles sopor and Eli, quoted above, embraced the Second Life affordance to obscure their disability identity, yet their comments in these quotes fail to consider the origins of the disabling social attitudes that they describe encountering in real life and the role that disability visibility plays in reversing this effect.

Wheelies creator Stevens explains his somewhat controversial choice to manifest as a wheelchair-using, helmet-wearing avatar, insisting that he did not want to be someone else:

> *I don't know how to be non-disabled and I've never wanted to be. It's important people know, it's part of who I am, plus I'm a disability consultant in Second Life, too, so I've got to look the part.*
>
> *Smith (2012)*

As Smith (2012) notes, different types of users with disability inhabit Second Life. Augmentationists, like Stevens, seek to represent themselves as authentically as possible, and embrace symbols of disability such as wheelchairs, guide dogs, canes, and other elements. By comparison, immersionists such as Eli and Niles seek out alternative or parallel realities to their real-life selves. These identity decisions are interesting in a virtual environment such as Second Life where users can walk, run, fly, and even teleport. The late disability activist and academic Christopher Newell described standing up and stepping away from his wheelchair as one of the most offensive things he could do in a public space (Goggin & Newell, 2003). In contrast, this is an entirely acceptable thing to do in Second Life and regularly happens as people dance in Wheelies. Against this backdrop, this chapter explores the intersection between disability identity, live music, and social inclusion at Wheelies during its "heyday" of 2006–2008.

Wheelies can be thought of as a kind of living or "live" media text that offers a specific representation of disability, at a specific moment in time, with live DJs providing the soundtrack. Just as disability, theories have turned repeatedly to a particular canon of disability films—for example, *The Best Years of Our Lives* (1946), *Coming Home* (1978), *Born on the Fourth of July* (1989), *My Left Foot* (1989), and more recently *Murderball* (2005) and *Avatar* (2010)—the Second Life nightclub drastically reconfigured disability community and representation, therefore making it worthy of critical reflection despite the virtual world and economy not living up to early media excitement expressed in the lead-up to the global financial crisis of late 2008.

The presence of a person in the virtual world as an avatar has two interrelated aspects as Schultze and Leahy (2009) note: "(i) telepresence: the sense of being there and (ii) social presence: the sense of being together with others." In Second Life, people can communicate both through text-based chat and also through voice. The virtual world has a number of different layers of sound. Besides the sound of other avatars' voices, it allows for ambient noise, music, and other effects produced by the world. These layers are linked to a particular avatar's presence within the virtual space—for example, a person speaking to the left of your avatar will sound as though they are standing to your left. Avatars that are further away will become inaudible. Sounds add to both the telepresence and social presence of a person in the world. These layers of sound also allow for music to be played both live in the world and also remediated for broadcast in that world, so audiences and performers share a sense of place and presence. As Schultze and Leahy (2009) observe, practices such as "sitting in a chair or dancing with someone, give communications a sense of being there and of being immersed and involved in the virtual events and spaces." Transformations occur in these spaces where an analog body is absent, but a digital body is a key part of a person's interaction with others and the world.

Digital live music can be played on a radio, although as Beers and Geesin (2009) note, "there is an ambiguity of time and place that accompanies these more mediated experiences of musical performance." The presence of digital live music in Second Life gives it a sense of place and a social presence that the virtual world enables, both between performers and their audience, and among members of the audience who share the experience of a performance. In this context, the identity of all participants takes on a particular significance, especially in Second Life where how an individual appears is an active choice on their part. This choice, in the context of Wheelies, brings a political statement about visibility and inclusion for people with disabilities to the dance floor, where the proclamation is accomplished by both the audience and the performers. Wheelies provides the place and timing—the event through which this politics is enacted by community members through avatars. For Sean Ebare (2005), music is related to identity and difference—subcultures emerge around musical tastes, practices, and subgenres. Music can provide the missing sensory cues in the online communication environments that people seek out to declare marginalized identities, such as disability. Wheelies has moved to a number of locations on the Second Life grids over the course of the club's existence, but its importance is as the shared presence of those who visit rather than its specific location. It can be anywhere on the main grid Agni; what is important is the place it represents, the social presence it enables, and through this, its ability to embody the music and performance—to make "live" the digital music, performed and heard by many different individuals, each alone at their computer screen.

Throughout this chapter, we examine three interrelated themes. Firstly, the role of media outside Second Life, both to promote the club and to propagate the political message of inclusion and acceptance the venue represents. Wheelies has been heavily profiled in mainstream media and has become a symbol of disability community creation and social inclusion, both in the media and academic publications. A second area is the role of live music to create and maintain a sense of social presence and telepresence among people who visit the club. Finally the role of choice and the use of avatar identity—by performers, the audience, and dancers—in further enabling a sense of shared presence and telepresence, and the politics that this realization embodies.

The chapter draws on the theoretical framework of "exuberant flourishing" offered by critical disability theorist Rosemary Garland-Thomson (2007), who builds an analysis of music into social and cultural models of disability. According to the social model, disability exists in inaccessible and inadaptable social practices that prevent the full inclusion of people that have impairments (Oliver, 1996). Exuberant flourishing emphasizes stories possible because of, rather than in spite of, disability, and offer a counter to traditional stories which focus on "despair, catastrophe, loss, excess, suffering, and relentless cure-seeking." Garland-Thomson (2007) identifies the importance of community and shared associations around a disability theme:

> *The human communities that form through deliberate or situational association in which shared experience bonds people together in mutually sustaining groups [is a primary site of exuberant flourishing]. Disability is seldom understood in our culture as the kind of experience that would lead to circles of supportive association based on commonality. Because we think of disability as at once individualized and isolating rather than communal and shared, the concept of a disability community in which one might thrive seems counterintuitive.*

In other words, exuberant flourishing means being proud of and flaunting disability as a strategy for social change and cultural recognition. These concepts are particularly relevant to music and dancing which, as Headlam (2006) explains, afford us the opportunity to engage in activities considered socially unacceptable in other situations:

> *When listening to music, we often have the feeling that our consciousness is altered. Our sense of the passing of time becomes highly experiential, following the twists and turns of the tempi and rhythms. [...] We can engage in all sorts of behaviors (clapping, dancing, shaking, head-banging etc.) that would be considered strange in the absence of music. It can be a shock when the "real" world impinges on our altered state; the musical world is a compelling place to be, and it serves many purposes.*

Garland-Thomson (2006) sketches a description of a group of academics with disabilities dancing at a disability studies conference dinner in real life as an example of exuberant flourishing:

> *The dance floor is a tangle of equipment and human variation [...] all roused to the beat of the music. Some of us lunge around; others glide smoothly on wheels; crutches prop some of us and stomp to the rhythm; still others fan white canes around them as if marking turf; the dogs rest quietly under the tables; people sip alternately on cocktails and wheelchair puff sticks to move around the room. Sign language criss-crosses the room, reaching through the loud music. Those of us with plenty of involuntary movement, the kind they struggled to keep under wraps in the workaday world, let it go where it may at the dance, twitching, bobbing, and jerking in distinctive patterns that anywhere else would make them targets of derision. [...] Everybody dances with everybody else—all partners in this lively violation of ordinary dance decorum. We proudly parade our differences with abandon. No self-consciousness here.*

For Garland-Thomson, the disabled academics' embrace of their irregular bodies signals an important corporeal moment in reinscribing disability in our cultural fabric. Their bodies proudly violate "ordinary dance decorum" in this welcoming space. Garland-Thomson describes a political intermixing of difference that would be a confronting image in another place. The dance floor, however, provided a place of exuberant flourishing through which to enact a performance of disability pride and culture.

Similarly, Wheelies is famous for its dance floor full of people's avatars both in and out of wheelchairs, some with virtual guide dogs, dancing and socializing together. The virtual dance floor is also a mix of human variation and exuberant flourishing. Avatars, as digital proxies for real people, display differences such as with wheelchairs, guide dogs, canes, and even wings. Wheelies offers another place for "no self-consciousness" and provides opportunity to reflect on the question of "what might happen to live music when the material and spatial dimensions are opened up to reworking as the boundaries and practicalities of the 'real' world are removed" (Beers & Geesin, 2009). Unlike a disability studies conference in the real world, Wheelies exists in an environment where a person can easily change their clothes, appearance, gender, race, and any virtual assistive devices associated with disability, with the click of a mouse. The remediation of live music and dancing through Second Life allows for both a more diverse and inclusive audience, but also for the message and politics it is enacting to be more widely distributed by leveraging on Second Life and Stevens' media profile.

7.1 Second Life: looking forward, looking back

Before we proceed, it is important to understand a little about Second Life and its history. The virtual world is hosted online and developed by Linden Lab in San Francisco. Second Life is a three-dimensional world rendered on a user's computer screen, much like popular online games such as World of Warcraft. However, the 3D space of Second Life has some significant differences. It is not a game; there is no way to win, and there is no overt contest with other people in the world. Rather it is a shared social place online. Second Life allows its users, known as residents, to create their own avatars which represent them in the virtual world. The world itself is also made up of what the residents have made there, from castles in the sky to detailed recreations of the Sistine Chapel. In 2013, Second Life celebrated its tenth anniversary, with the theme for the celebrations "looking forward, looking back." Looking forward, looking back makes for an interesting focus. Second Life, which is free to use, has a relatively stable population of about a million residents, and an in-game gross domestic product of about $US750 million (Lacy, 2012).

While it has made substantial achievements over a 10-year period, looking forward, the platform is not going to challenge Facebook. However, looking back to the hype around Second Life in its media halcyon days of 2006–2008, this would seem hard to believe. In 2006 Second Life was twice the cover story on *Business Week* (Hof, 2006a,b), the second time to excitedly announce the world's first resident to have amassed a million dollars in virtual assets. The next year, musician Suzanne Vega (2007) wrote an article for *Time* magazine listing Linden's founder Philip Rosedale as one of the top 100 most influential people in the world. Lampe (2012) characterizes 2007 for Second Life as "the peak of inflated expectations." This outlook was arguably driven by the mainstream media, which offered strong emphasis on the potential for Second Life as a commercial place. Reuters had a reporter based in Second Life, while Sony, IBM, and nearly one in seven other Fortune 500 companies had a visible presence in the world (Barnetta, 2009). Management consultants McKinsey & Company warned that companies would ignore virtual worlds such as Second Life "at their peril" (Richards, 2008). The future of the web was described as being three-dimensional, and the possibility that virtual worlds might one day supplant the existing text-based platforms was considered a real possibility (Vernon, Lewis, & Lynch, 2009). Universities and hospitals began buying virtual land with the aim of offering services in the world. However, it soon became apparent that the media hype had led to a larger audience and media profile than would have been possible just through the actual number of people in the world (Marshall, 2011). It is illustrative that in 2008 both the Reuters reporter left Second Life and Stevens resigned as Wheelies manager.

Second Life and Wheelies in particular represent a crucial moment in the evolution of people with disabilities' use of, and representation in, online spaces. Wheelies offered a reconfiguration of virtual life, cultural practices, and the manifestation of a previously spurned identity, disability. As Beers and Geesin (2009) note, "Second Life's potential to drastically reconfigure virtual culture—and for that matter, cultural artifacts, events, and practices in more general terms—means that it is worth critical reflection in its own right." The Second Life world allows people a lot of freedom to create whatever they want, and have an avatar that appears in many different forms, with the virtual world's website announcing its slogan: "Your imagination, your world." However, as Beers and Geesin (2009) point out, much of Second Life's grid consists of constructions that are trying to recreate the real. Similarly, Boellstorff (2008) found that many Second Life norms and social practices come from the actual world. Schechtman (2012) observed that for a small but significant number of residents, their avatars are as real for them and as much a part of themselves as their analog bodies. This connection between Second Life and the real world is reflected in Stevens' comments about his desire to reflect the markers of what he believes communicates his disabled identity from the actual world (Smith, 2012). Stevens' disabled identity was crucial to both his telepresence and his social presence. His somewhat unexpected choice in trying to represent the real and include people with disabilities was a political act.

7.2 Identity avatars and disability

Questions of identity and the Internet have a long history. A famous New Yorker cartoon from Peter Steiner depicts two dogs sitting in front of a computer, with one commenting to the other, "On the internet, no-one knows you are a dog." This was first published in 1993, a decade before Second Life, and before the World Wide Web had become part of people's everyday life. As Dobransky and Hargittai (2006) observe:

> *The most striking aspect of online communication for people with disabilities is the ability it affords the user to hide aspects of him—or herself. For people with disabilities, online communication may allow the removal of their disability from the forefront of the interaction.*

However, with some impairments, it will be easier to avoid disclosure than with others. For wheelchair users, this may be just a question of avatar design; however, for others, such as people with cognitive, vision, or hearing impairment who require accessibility measures that may force disclosure, particularly if they are unavailable, disability remains at the forefront. As Best and Butler (2013) found, the role of the physical body can act to limit the actions of the avatar body by making it difficult for a person to interact with the technology. Before Second Life activated its voice communication, deaf people were able to use the network easily through the text interface; however, they were excluded when the new technology was deployed and residents increasingly moved to the new communications medium (Carr, 2009). Similarly people with a vision impairment will find access far more problematic, although there has been considerable work done to make Second Life more accessible for this group, including the design of the virtual guide dogs seen in Wheelies that interpret the virtual world for people who are using a screen reader (Smith, 2012).

These questions of identity, representation, and accessibility remain just as relevant in the context of Second Life where your digital proxy can *actually* be a dog. Jones (2006) observes that people are judged by their avatars in Second Life, just as they are by their bodies in real life, although in the virtual world it is easy to change bodies, and people can and do change their avatars' appearance and whole body for different situations and locations. As one of the Second Life residents interviewed in Tom Boellstorff's (2008) anthropological study of the grid commented, "I've come to observe that the outward appearance really does communicate a lot about who you are, because it's made up of conscious choices about how you want to present yourself." Boellstorff (2008) observes that people with disabilities fear that discrimination does not disappear within a virtual embodiment. Hudson (2007) interviewed a resident of Second Life who is a wheelchair user in real life about her experiences in the virtual world:

> *I find the attitude of people in Second Life to people with disabilities [is disappointing]. I have run an experiment myself. I've gone to this particular website as an able-bodied person, got out on the dance floor and danced for half an hour with different avatars or different people, or whatever you call them. Then I've gone away, put myself in my wheelchair, gone back, the same people were there and they didn't want to know me.*

There are approximately 1 million active Second Life residents (Lacy, 2012), about 25% of whom could have a disability (Smith, 2012). In the virtual world, residents appear as their avatars. These virtual representations of people can take on many forms. When you first sign up for the game, it offers a choice of starter virtual bodies, including humans, vampires, animals, robots, and vehicles. However, the majority of residents present as some form of human, often as idealized versions of themselves (Boellstorff, 2008). As Jones (2006) observes, "unlike the real world, *Second Life* users are not stuck with the body that they are given, but can remake or create their body, however, they wish." Stevens (2011) describes being forced to initially manifest as nondisabled but then remaking his body as he developed literacy in the world:

> *While there were already wheelchair in Secondlife (sl), I believe they were only designed for demonstration purposes and it was never perceived that would be used fulltime as who would want to be disabled in sl? Well as someone who has always had cerebral palsy from birth, which affected my mobility amongst other things I wanted people to see what I was a disabled person. Since in sl, our appearances as avatars is our representation of who we are I did not feel comfortable appearing as a nondisabled person as I would have to keep explaining that I was not a nondisabled person which would be hard to comprehend without a wheelchair.*

Stevens adds that over time he added a helmet to his avatar to gain an even more faithful representation of his real-life self. When Stevens initially joined Second Life, it was not easy to equip an avatar with a wheelchair; the process of gradually adding to his disability identity, in world, by acquiring symbols of his real-life self was vital because he wanted people to know about his disability identity so he would not have to explain it to them. As Boellstorff (2008) notes, the virtual world's structural predisposition toward physically perfect, youthful-looking avatars meant people with disabilities were not immediately apparent and they could amass a number of in-world friends who could know them for months without knowing that they had any impairments. However, the relationship between an individual and their avatar in Second Life changes in different circumstances. As Schultze and Leahy (2009) observe:

> *It is important to remember that identity boundaries are socially constructed and situated. This suggests that the avatar-self relationship is not binary—either integrated or segmented—but multi-dimensional and located at different points of the continuum at different points in time.*

Wheelies' focus on inclusion offered a reworking of identity boundaries. Stevens challenged the existing norms of virtual identity through his insistence on appearing as disabled, and through his in-world popularity as well as his desire to establish one of the "hottest clubs" in Second Life, that, although a mainstream club, promoted disability inclusion. Creating a nightclub as a locus for inclusion is significant because at the time, Second Life was an immersive environment heralded as offering the potential for a "richer mediation of live events" in the context of live music performance (Beers & Geesin, 2009).

7.3 Second Life, live music, and disability

Sant (2009) finds that "a growing number of musicians, theater makers and other performers are exploring Second Life as a stage for their ideas," while Beers and Geesin (2009) observe that Second Life brings audience and performer together. There is no need to book venues and, importantly, the performer and each member of the audience do not have to be in the same physical place; they are able to link through the virtual world from all over the planet, yet the performer is still able to receive feedback from listeners. Second Life offers a democratizing platform as Beers and Geesin (2009) note: "the wide gap between listener and performer is erased." In this context the real-time—live—nature of the performance is what gives this interaction its allure.

The intersection of disability and music is about identity and visibility, creating and demanding a space (Cameron, 2009). Live music was an important feature in the disability arts movement of the 1980s and 1990s and also integral to the success of Wheelies. Stevens (2011) explains that Wheelies' beginnings were "small and basic," with a few friends dancing to the radio. However, changes began taking place very quickly and Wheelies opened as a full-blown nightclub with "a grand event including DJing from Cher Harrington, live music from Kazoo Twang followed by fireworks." This event clearly draws on the approach taken by real-world nightclub openings when managers engage well-known DJs and performers to attract a crowd in the hopes of becoming the hottest place in town. The choice of artists represents the different types of digital live music that Wheelies embraced. Cher Harrington is a famous DJ in Second Life who supports creating opportunities for live artists, while Kazoo Twang is a popular Second Life singer and cabaret performer. The replication of real-world nightclub practices helped to establish Wheelies, but so too did the focus on disability social change.

7.4 Wheelies, live music, and engagement

Smith and Aaker (2010) argue that there are four principles of engagement to leverage social media for social change. Each of these principles intersects with Wheelies' use of live music for disability inclusion within what is a "mainstream club" (Stevens, personal communication, 2013). The first step, according to Smith and Aaker, is telling a story. Stories help us understand life, with the story of disability having been told in a particular ways, to make sense of humanity and the human condition. As Lerner and Strauss observe:

> *Once one starts to think about music through the lens of disability, disability suddenly appears everywhere—in the bodies and minds of composers and performers, in the reception histories of musical works, and even in the works themselves, embedded there in the form of persistent narratives.*
>
> *Lerner and Strauss (2006)*

According to Garland-Thomson (2006), disability "saturates [our] cultural fabric" and has been most often understood as a "medical pathology or individual inadequacy." Indeed, disability structures many types of narratives. As Joseph Straus (2011) explains, "music is able to tell stories, and among the stories it tells are stories about disability." He finds that the "overcoming all odds" narrative trajectory has influenced cultural understandings of the intersections between music and disability. However, Stevens and Wheelies offered a different story, a story of disability pride. This pride took place on the dance floor and behind the turntable, through the live performers and audience. The very presence of disabled patrons and DJs was a new story that resonated with people with disabilities, those without, and the mainstream media. Stevens as the nightclub's manager and his patrons created personal stories of disability inclusion through their avatars, both through their appearance and actions. As Jensen (2009) observes, "actors create a personal story and history of their avatar that transforms them into the mediators of being in the virtual world, and also how the avatars act as the mediators that transform the actors themselves."

A key feature of storytelling, according to Smith and Aaker, is focusing on a protagonist who seems "real so that the audience begins to feel a stake in what happens." Stevens has been quoted many times as saying he did not want to manifest within Second Life as nondisabled when having a disability was so integral to his personality. His vision for Wheelies was not so much as having a disability-specific place but to have a club that was broadly inclusive and disability friendly. Wheelies, specifically through the medium of live music and dance, was an early challenge to the idea that the Internet allowed nondisclosure of disability and that is what people with disabilities wanted—and, by extension, rhetoric that this was empowering. Wheelies' move from a group of people listening to the radio together to live music illustrates the importance of space and community, particularly within the context of disability inclusion. Live music gave Wheelies a legitimate status as a mainstream nightclub. As an online space portraying identity, Wheelies also offered the opportunity to embrace, not hide, disability. This is a radical notion that was able to remediate disability.

Polgara Paine, Wheelies' manager after Stevens, maintains that the club did not want a disabled community, but rather an inclusive community (Hickey-Moody & Wood, 2010). The club employed people who identified as disabled, including a manager, DJ, and a landscape gardener. This leads us to Smith and Aaker's second point regarding social change through social media: get people to empathize. The most important reason people become engaged with another person's goal is personal relevance. It is clear throughout his interviews and blog posts that Wheelies was important to Stevens; he was passionate about the disability cause and providing an inclusive venue that also provided great live music. This represents the third design principle in creating a social movement: being authentic. People empathized with Stevens and, by extension, Wheelie's quest for social inclusion; perhaps they empathized with his experience of not fitting in, with his drive for disability inclusion, or maybe just his love of live music performance. For example, Duilio Cimino, a Wheelies patron, who has multiple sclerosis in real life and uses a wheelchair in Second Life but stands to dance at Wheelies, comments, "[Wheelies] is super and good music" (Semyorka, 2007). Smith and Aaker recommend stressing similarities with your target in order to create an instant connection. While people may not have experience of Stevens' impairment, the link to a nightclub, and dancing to live music, creates a commonality that allows for the idea of inclusion for people with disabilities in such a place. This message then resonates and is shared beyond Second Life to an audience of people who, while unlikely to visit the virtual world, are able to understand the message that Wheelies represents.

Smith and Aaker's fourth design principle is "match the media." By this they mean choose the media that will most empower your target. They encourage people and groups that are seeking to effect social change to think about the media platform they adopt. For Stevens, Second Life was the obvious choice because he believed the immersive environment in which things could be achieved in such a short period of time offered him the potential to realize his own "aims and goals" (2011). The nightclub was similarly significant because it represented a mainstream environment, but with a twist:

> *The reason I decided I needed a nightclub within my Second Life "portfolio" was that it is an era where everyone was owning and running nightclubs in the circles I was in, and so I wanted one! Since I was disabled, I thought it would be fun to have a disability themed club. It was never intended to be just for disabled people and at the time I was the only disabled user I knew.*
>
> *Stevens (2011)*

Although Stevens concedes that other social media platforms have taken on a prominent disability presence, he told us he believes "SL is still ahead of the game," suggesting the technology itself is not yet powerful enough to ensure its mainstream status in our lives (personal communication, 2013). The two simple ideas of Wheelies and Stevens using a wheelchair in Second Life, he believes, "demonstrated not only what Second Life can do for disabled people but also what disabled people can do for Second Life."

Smith and Aaker (2010) also recommend leveraging offline media. Wheelies was the most profiled Second Life nightclub in the mainstream media. Leveraging on the back of the high level of interest in Second Life, Wheelies was the story that showed the type of things that could be done or were possible in this virtual world. This allowed for both the popularity and profile of the club to provide a spiral of interest, but also an avenue for the political message the club embodied to be deployed more widely. The virtual space that Wheelies housed brought performers, DJs, and the audience together, with the live music creating an enhanced sense of social copresence and individual telepresence. While this occurred at other nightclubs in Second Life, at Wheelies it was vitally important because it initiated a sense of disability inclusion. The creation of a disabled identity by Stevens and many of his patrons was an overtly political act. It was at once both an example of what an accessible space in real life could be and a message about inclusion in the Second Life grid and the Internet in general.

7.5 Conclusion

The launch of Wheelies in 2006 attracted a high level of media interest in Second Life and disability inclusion. Wheelies as a wheelchair-themed mainstream nightclub was first conceived as a side project for a Second Life-based disability training center. While the club still operates, Stevens (2011) describes 2007 as the club's heyday. As with Second Life, much of the inflated buzz around Wheelies came through the media in real life, and particularly through Stevens acting as a spokesperson and advocate. Mirroring Second Life itself, publicity and media in the real world drove a higher level of activity and engagement with the virtual world.

Wheelies and Simon Stevens represent a radically different approach to identity online, and specifically in Second Life. Stevens' refusal to adopt a "perfect" avatar, electing instead to reflect his real-life reality, created a social movement that people empathized with in the community. Stevens notes he did not feel comfortable appearing as a nondisabled person, explaining to Hickey-Moody and Wood (2010), "I haven't got time to be someone else." This display of identity by Stevens and Wheelies staff and patrons is a political act that challenges existing models of disability and identity, and promotes inclusion both in Second Life and beyond.

These displays of identity at Wheelies need the catalyst of the club itself. Wheelies provided a social presence for the different people involved, acting as a pretense for their interactions. The live music that flows through the club via performers and DJs is the essential element of the club, as is the club to the music, bringing audience and performers together in the virtual world and linking them through their individual computers. By dancing to the music, avatars' act of display and exuberant flourishing provided a message, a story to tell beyond the virtual confines of Second Life grid. The message is conveyed in the displaying identity, in the form of interaction, if not in the content of the music itself.

References

Barnetta, A. (2009). *Fortune 500 companies in Second Life: Activities, their success measurement and the satisfaction level of their projects*. Master's Thesis, ETH Zurich. Retrieved from http://www.smi.ethz.ch/education/thesis/Barnetta_SecondLife.pdf.

Beers, D. & Geesin, B. (2009). Rockin' with the avatars: "Live" music and the virtual spaces of Second Life. In D. Heider (Ed.), *Living virtually: Researching new worlds*. New York: Peter Lang.

Best, K. & Butler, S. (2013). Second Life avatars as extensions of social physical bodies in people with myalgic encephalomyelitis/chronic fatigue syndrome. *Continuum: Journal of Media & Cultural Studies*, 27(3), 837–849.

Boellstorff, T. (2008). *Coming of age in Second Life: An anthropologist explores the virtually human*. Princeton and Oxford: Princeton University Press.

Cameron, C. (2009). Tragic but brave or just crips with chips? Songs and their lyrics in the disability arts movement in Britain. *Popular Music*, 3, 381–396.

Carr, D. (2009). Virtually accessible. *Access: The inclusive design journal*, 23–25, Spring.

Cassidy, M. (2007). Flying with disability in Second Life. *Eureka Street*, 17(8). Retrieved from http://www.eurekastreet.com.au/article.aspx?aeid=2787#.UaxhCdjVDCo.

Dobransky, K. & Hargittai, E. (2006). The disability divide in Internet access and use. *Information Communication and Society*, 9(3), 313–334.

Ebare, S. (2005). Digital music and subculture: Sharing files, sharing styles. *First Monday*, 9(2). http://firstmonday.org/issues/issue9_2/ebare/index.html.

Friedkin, K. (2008). Accessibility & Second Life. *Grid Life*. http://www.kippiefriedkin.com/2008/09/11/accessibility-second-life.

Garland-Thomson, R. (2006). Foreword. In N. Lerner & J. Straus (Eds.), *Sounding off: Theorizing disability in music*. New York and London: Routledge.

Garland-Thomson, R. (2007). Shape structures story: Fresh and feisty stories about disability. *Narrative*, 15(1), 113–123.

Goggin, G. & Newell, C. (2003). *Digital disability: The social construction of disability in new media*. Lanham: Rowman and Littlefield Publishers Inc.

Headlam, D. (2006). Learning to hear autistically. In N. Lerner & J. Straus (Eds), *Sounding off: Theorizing disability in music*. New York and London: Routledge.

Hickey-Moody, A. & Wood, D. (2010). Ethics in Second Life: Difference, desire and the production of subjectivity. In C. Wankel & S. Malleck (Eds), *Emerging ethical issues of life in virtual worlds*. United States of America: IAP—Information Age Publishing.

Hof, R. (2006a). My virtual life. *Business Week*, 30 April, Retrieved from http://www.businessweek.com/stories/2006-04-30/my-virtual-life.

Hof, R. (2006b). Second Life's first millionaire. *Business Week*, 26 November, Retrieved from http://www.businessweek.com/the_thread/techbeat/archives/2006/11/second_lifes_fi.html.

Hudson, R. (2007). Wheeling in Second Life. *Web Usability*, Retrieved from http://usability.com.au/2007/12/wheeling-in-second-life.

Jensen, S. S. (2009). Actors and their use of avatars as personal mediators: An empirical study of avatar-based sense-making and communication practice in the virtual worlds of Everquest and Second Life. *MediaKulture: Journal of Media and Communications Research*, 25(47), 29–44. Retrieved from http://ojs.statsbiblioteket.dk/index.php/mediekultur/article/view/1403.

Jones, D. E. (2006). Avatar: constructions of self and place in Second Life and the technological imagination. *Gnovis*, 6, 1–32. Retrieved from http://gnovisjournal.org/files/Donald-E-Jones-I-Avatar.pdf.

Lacy, S. (2012). *Philip Rosedale: The media is wrong, Second Life didn't fail*. PandoDaily, 6 July. Retrieved from http://pandodaily.com/2012/07/06/philip-rosedale-the-media-is-wrong-secondlife-didnt-fail.

Lampe, C. (2012). Virtual worlds: Promise and pitfalls. *UAE Journal of Educational Technology and E-Learning*. Retrieved from http://ejournal.hct.ac.ae/article/virtual-worlds.

Lerner, N. & Strauss, J. (2006). Introduction. In N. Lerner & J. Straus (Eds), *Sounding off: Theorizing disability in music*. New York and London: Routledge.

Marshall, G. (2011). Whatever happened to Second Life? *Techradar*, 30 September. Retrieved from http://www.techradar.com/au/news/internet/whatever-happened-to-second-life-1030314.

Oliver, M. (1996). *Understanding disability: From theory to practice*. Hampshire: Palgrave.

Richards, J. (2008). *McKinsey: Ignore Second Life at your peril*. Times Online. Retrieved from http://www.mohr-mohr-and-more.org/services/environnements-virtuels/20-conseils-et-services/mondes-virtuels/23-mckinsey-ignore-second-life-at-your-peril-english-only.

Sant, T. (2009). Chapter 10: Performance in Second Life: some possibilities for learning and teaching. In J. Molka-Danielsen & M. Deutchhmann (Eds), *Learning and teaching in the virtual world of Second Life*. Trondheim: Tapir Academic Press.

Schechtman, M. (2012). The story of my Second Life: Virtual worlds and narrative identity. *Philosophy and Technology*, 25(3), 329–343.

Schultze, U. & Leahy, M. M. (2009). The avatar-self relationship: Enacting presence in Second Life. In *In the proceedings of the international conference on information systems (ICIS), Phoenix, Arizona*. Retrieved from http://sled.577505.n2.nabble.com/attachment/5575195/0/PresenceISL.pdf.

Semyorka, S. (2007). *Empowering the physically challenged* (2nd edition). Retrieved from http://secondedition.wordpress.com/2007/07/28/empowering-the-physically-challenged.

Smith, K. (2012). Universal life: the use of virtual worlds among people with disabilities. *Universal Access Information Society*, 11, 387–398.

Smith, A. & Aaker, J. (2010). *The dragonfly effect: Quick, effective and powerful ways to use social media for social change*. San Francisco: Jossey-Bass, a Wiley Imprint.

Stevens, S. (2011). *The Wheelies story*. Retrieved from http://issuu.com/simonstevens74/docs/wheeliesstory/8?e=2224897/2921921.

Stevens, S. (2013). Personal interview.

Straus, J. (2011). *Extraordinary measures: Disability in music*. Oxford: Oxford University Press.

Vega, S. (2007). *The 2007 Time 100: Builders and titans, Philip Rosedale*. Time Magazine. Retrieved from http://www.time.com/time/specials/2007/time100/article/0,28804,1595326_1615737_1615877,00.html.

Vernon, R., Lewis, L., & Lynch, D. (2009). Virtual worlds and social work education: Potentials for "Second Life". *Advances in Social Work*, 10(2), 176–192, Fall.

Voodoo, B. (2008). SecondLife SingaLong. *Rez Magazine*. Retrieved from http://rezmagazine.blogspot.com.au/2008/08/secondlife-singalong.html.

The sounds of Skyrim: a musical journey through gaming

8

S. Gallacher

8.1 Introduction

We're the children of Skyrim, and we fight all our lives
And when Sovngarde beckons, every one of us dies
We drink to our youth, for days come and gone
For the Age of Aggression is just about done

Age of Aggression, *Skyrim*

I recently attended a screening of the film *The Lord of the Rings: Fellowship of the Ring* accompanied by the Western Australian Symphony Orchestra playing the entire film score live to the audience. A full choir of more than 120 singers participated, creating a powerful and emotional rendition of this soundtrack compiled especially for Peter Jackson's epic film trilogy by J.R.R. Tolkien. This sold-out event demonstrated two phenomena: the exposure of a new audience, namely science fiction and fantasy fans, to the classical music genre; and the classical music audience embracing the incorporation of popular culture into a traditional framework. At this live concert, two distinct audiences were joining together to share the experience, and the result was engaging, emotional, and captivating. The *Lord of the Rings* live concert is a phenomenon emerging distinctly out of the digital realm. A hallmark of the cinematic trilogy was its use of cutting-edge digital film technologies. This resulted in a filmic identity, which embedded practices of digital engagement while maintaining a visceral connection to its audience that many previous Computer Generated Imagery (CGI) films had struggled to achieve. The films, and the live symphonies which followed, demonstrate a way in which the digital can be fertile, fecund, and organic in their emergence and growth. As the realm of the digital grows, it is not surprising that its presence will be increasingly revealed in more diverse and dynamic ways. In particular, the world of digital games, a space which has grown in popularity in the past three decades, is making its impact felt far beyond the personal computer, console, or mobile gaming device.

The rise of digital gaming has seen an overwhelming deluge of creativity and innovation as computer games evolve into increasingly complex and interactive sites of activity. An emerging field of academic thought muses on the growth of "video games" as a body of cultural (inter)activity (Mark & Perron, 2003; Jesper, 2005; King & Krzywinska, 2006). The integration of networked technologies has further fuelled this growth as players interact with each other, both within the game environment, and outside of it in the form of fan-based communities. These digital markers could be seen

The Digital Evolution of Live Music

to signal a retreat from the "real" as we dwell in increasingly virtual spaces. Much has been written about the transformation of human interaction in favor of online and virtual relationships (Rheingold, 1993; Turkle, 1997), raising concerns that our transgressions into the virtual world result in disconnection, abstraction, and a loss of interpersonal complexity (Ellison & Boyd, 2013).

By contrast, however, network computing has allowed players to converge in communal environments and interact in real-time. Gaming environments such as Multi-User Domains (MUDs) and Massively Multiplayer Online Role-Playing Games (MMORPGs)[1] like *World of Warcraft* and *Everquest II* provide a platform where people in the same room or across the planet can connect in a shared environment to play. Gaming environments of this nature are comprised of many qualities which constitute a "live" experience. It is the concept of liveness as a primarily "temporal relationship, a relationship of simultaneity" that is significant here (Auslander, 2002, p. 21). Real-time interaction, group quests and missions requiring collaboration and cooperation, and events where a global audience logs in to participate at dedicated times are just some of the features of this type of virtual-live experience. In the same way that music fans are turning the concept of "live" on its head, gamers are transforming the live: "even though they are not physically present, and are in different time zones, fans are gathering to share their opinions and knowledge … in such a way that they not only feel part of the 'live' music experience, but also create their own" Bennett (2013, p. 548). This emergence of the "live" gaming experience has in recent times—through a range of games, including online multiplayer and single player—revealed a new version of the live and, in particular, live music.

This chapter explores digital gaming and the role of live music within the realms of the game and its more recent overflow into "Real Life"[2] (RL). In particular, the reproduction of musical scores, created as soundtracks to digital games, being performed live in the analog settings of RL signals a significant shift in the relationship between digital culture and live music. This dynamic brings into focus the growing legitimacy of digital games—as recreation, as social spaces of interaction and as sites of creative endeavor created in collaborative, interactive networks. It simultaneously reinvigorates live music as a participatory space for a new or re-energized fan base—the digital gaming demographic. Considering the role of music in the game Skyrim, alongside my subjective experience as a gamer participating in the Skyrim universe, this chapter illustrates the creation of a feedback loop; mutually defining and reinforcing connections between gaming culture and live music enhance meaning, simulation, and recollection of gaming experiences while reshaping what constitutes "live." These connections are creating a new genre of RL live musical performance and a new live music experience "in-game." RL live music experiences of gaming music generate a musical trigger for evoking and remembering in-game experiences and this, in turn, highlights an increasingly interdependent relationship between live, virtual, and real.

[1] MMORPG stands for Massively Multiplayer Online Role-Playing Game. The MMO indicates the game is played via a network in which you are interacting with real players across the globe.

[2] A definition of "Real Life" is given by Anna Peachey in "Reinventing ourselves: Contemporary concepts of identity in virtual worlds" (2011), p. 46: "some distinguish it as 'first life' rather than 'real'...".

8.2 The music of Skyrim

In 2011, Bethesda Game Studios released Skyrim (Chapter 5 in the Elder Scrolls saga). Widely lauded as the best single-player game of the year (Severino, 2011; PC Gamer, 2012; BloodReaper, 2012), its special "Legendary Edition" release notes on its cover state that it is the "winner of over 200 Game of the Year titles." Skyrim is an action Role-Playing Game (RPG) centered on a created character's battle against a dragon, Alduin. Skyrim, a geographical location, is an "open-world" game design, meaning the player is free to explore and interact with the sprawling maps of the game world in any way they choose. This leads to a sense of the individual carving their own in-game experience, rather than being directed down particular pathways (literally and figuratively). This style of gameplay, emphasising independence and self-direction, is reliant on the creation of a world which, for gamers, is atmospheric, captivating, and worthy of exploration.

At the time of its release, Skyrim featured cutting-edge graphics, an enhanced user interface, and in-depth scriptwriting. It also contained original musical compositions, played in-game, to heighten effects and mood creation. Composed by Jeremy Soule, songs include *Dragonborn*, the game's main theme. *Dragonborn* was recorded with a choir of more than 30 people singing in the created in-game language, Draconic. The live quality of this composition arguably lent character and depth to the game, demonstrating that gaming is an emerging forum for artistic creativity.

Skyrim is by no means the first instance of games incorporating music into design, with soundtracks playing an important and increasing role in game composition since Taito's *Space Invaders* in 1978 (Collins, 2008). Since then the relationship between games and music has evolved into one of mutual definition where music in games is a significant component of the music industry. A new site for music consumption has emerged, with virtual and digital gaming origins. Simultaneously, the real-time interactivity of these sites means they can also be live. Thus, despite the seeming virtuality of digital gaming, liveness remains a significant component of the musical experience within games.

Musical scores and soundtracks are capable of profound impact on their audience. The ability to create mood, build suspense and invoke a spectrum of intense emotions can form the foundation of success in film and television. According to Bordwell and Thompson (1993), sound "engages another sense mode: our visual attention can be accompanied by aural attention" (p. 181). It creates links to the visual action unfolding, in an active relationship (p. 184). More recently, the power of music and sound within digital games has become increasingly apparent. Indeed, some of the particularities of digital games—such as the reduced emotive range of a computer generated character—can be enhanced and enriched with a powerful musical score.

Digital games take us to entirely new universes and realities, and they are more richly built and invoked when music accompanies the player in their journey to a new world. EVE Online, a MMORPG set in the vast infiniteness of space, is accompanied by a long, complex, and moving orchestral musical score. This game involves long-term play, often with long periods of time without "action," so the need for atmospheric music to build the context of the immensity of space adds to players' immersion and investment in the development of their character and its ship. The musical gaming journey has followed the player into RL, where strong gaming cultures, like those seen in Japan, have for decades now enjoyed traveling concerts of live performance showcasing video game music. Games like Konami's *Dane Dance Revolution* (DDR), where players match movement cursors on the screen with the movement of their own feet to create dance routines, have seen the rise of subcultures of "Web communities of informed music fans" (Demers, 2006, p. 402). Players of DDR select their own character before commencing play along with the type of music they want to dance to and its difficulty rating (p. 403). In doing so, individual players project onto the game screen a version of themselves with which they (wish to) identify. The trance-like and evocative nature of the game's electronic music is a critical part of creating a sense of identity, participation, and immersion in the game. DDR, like Skyrim and many other games, has witnessed a consonant explosion of online forums, fan sites, and subcultures that cater to those "in the know" to celebrate and re-enact moments experienced in-game.

8.2.1 Music in-game

Music within a game is also a marker of location in a (virtual) geographical sense. It operates in both diegetic and nondiegetic ways (Bordwell & Thompson, 1993). Diegetically, bards in local towns sing songs that contribute to building a sense of place, narrative, and community, evoking the classical "tavern" scene of a remote village. Nondiegetically, a musical soundscape pervades all parts of the Skyrim world, adding to the overall atmosphere being crafted in the game. Often, this music is the same as that played and sung by the bards in the villages, while their source is as yet unknown to the gamer traversing these broader landscapes beyond the clusters of villages and towns. Links between these diegetic and nondiegetic compositions weave a fabric of the song throughout the Skyrim landscape, creating a consistency of immersion and atmosphere in the universe. The song *Age of Aggression* appears in a slightly varied format as the *Age of Oppression*, to signify which "side" of the Skyrim universe you have chosen to base your character: the Stormcloaks hear the *Age of Oppression*, while the pro-Imperial variant hear the *Age of Aggression*. Upon entering an Imperial-controlled inn, it is not uncommon to hear a bard singing the *Age of Aggression* or similarly to hear the *Age of Oppression* when entering Stormcloak territory. If a battle has recently been won—for example, the Stormcloaks take control of an imperial city—the bards in those inns will begin to sing the *Age of Oppression* to recognise the victors. These diegetic audio markers add depth to the sense of "place" generated in-game. Outside of the game, a gamer playing one or the other version of this song indicates where their allegiance in Skyrim lies. It also evokes and invokes the moods and experiences of playing the game, transporting them into a "real life," or "out of game," context.

8.2.2 Music from the game

Despite their ability to add to the excitement and attachment to the game experience, in-game musical devices have largely remained a one-way transmission from sender to receiver. However, when Mexican-born singer Judith de los Santos (known as "Malukah") performed an acoustic version of Skyrim's theme, *Dragonborn Comes*, that was posted on YouTube in November 2011, the potential of digital culture as live music was revealed. Gathering 2 million views in two weeks (in 2014, it is now sitting at nearly 10 million plays), this haunting rendition of *Dragonborn Comes* demonstrates that digital gaming is capable of composing and producing beautiful music, worthy in its own right in RL, outside of the game. Malukah has since (re)produced other songs from Skyrim, and other games, including writing an original composition inspired by the game, Mass Effect, called *Reignite*.

Gamers now play Malukah's rendition of *Dragonborn Comes* on their mobile music devices, invoking and reinvoking their experience of their game play in the real world. Both the sophistication of the musical composition itself, coupled with the emotive memories it evokes in the replaying (and thus the retelling of their gaming story), combine to create a powerful musical experience for the listener. The gamer-generated "story" behind the music and the role the individual plays in creating, reliving, and retelling their individual and collective story while listening to game generated music creates a musical connection that is beyond merely listening to and enjoying music. The agency, interactivity, and control gamers have over their virtual characters and environments means they also feel like participants—cocreators of the musical meaning—because they heard a particular song when they chose to traverse a certain landscape or fight in a particular battle. In this way, gamers are a part of the performance—actors in the story of the gaming narrative, which includes the music that comprises its soundtrack.

8.3 Music and live-gaming experiences: a moment in time, a moment in mind

This digital connection to music in games has sent out tendrils into the world of popular music, communicating and celebrating stories of connection to a live audience. As gamers become embedded in the performance of a game, the relationship between the producer and the user is thoroughly blurred, resulting in a new identity, the 'produser' (Bruns, 2008) emerging, through these collaborative and dynamic interactions. What emerges from the gaming matrix is an environment where programmers, researchers, marketers, gamers, mappers, and modders converge into a complex and interactive network to create an experience in a nonlinear and ongoing fashion. This experience is then delivered to a broader "live" audience who hears the songs in RL as additional participants in this process.

There have been samples of *Dragonborn Comes* played at live concerts. One such example is the Dutch DJ team Headhunterz, who sampled both Malukah's acoustic and Soule's original game version of the song in their live concert, to the great delight of the Skyrim fans in the audience. Audience reaction to the samples evoked an RL communal experience where a specialised knowledge of the sample and its background demonstrated their belonging within a select group. Headhunterz have since released a single titled *Dragonborn Comes* as a tribute to Skyrim. Following this, Skyrim composer Jeremy Soule put out a call to his Facebook fans to assess their interest in a live concert of the Skyrim soundtrack, along with other compositions from Oblivion and Morrowind. He later posted that Malukah agreed to appear at a proposed New York concert and would join him onstage to sing her renditions of the popular gaming songs.

The reproduction of gaming music outside of the game environment allows the gamer to be transported back to their gaming experience in RL, in the way that perhaps only music is uniquely capable of doing. It recalls and invokes the tension, emotion, and excitement of in-game events and experiences, and positions them in a new light and a different space. Gamers describe the sensation of hearing the music of Skyrim being played "out of world" as a visceral one. When reproduced in a live setting, gamers also have the opportunity for shared knowledge to be expressed within a community of actual people, as opposed to gaming avatars, which spontaneously forms and then dissipates. This experience is distinctly "live" in the way that it is played at a particular time and place, literally in concert with others. The shared experience is at once dynamic and unique because of its evocative nature—conjuring and recalling a shared knowledge.

The ability of music to invoke a past gaming experience in a live experience, like the memories conjured up from a movie soundtrack, is not a new phenomenon. For decades, games have been designed with a steady attention to the role, timbre, and tone of music within the game. In a virtual environment, audio soundtracks contribute a powerful component to the world being created. The rise of adrenalin in climactic moments within games is assisted and enhanced by a well-created soundtrack—whether it is derived from original compositions or the insertion of popular music into digital games. The impact of these soundtracks remain with the player long after the game is played, completed, and put in a box never to be played again.

Considering the use of music in the film industry, it has long been understood that when building a virtual reality, music and sound are vital to the composition of the environment. For me, the song *Firestarter* by Prodigy will always conjure memories of playing the racing video game Wipeout 2097 on the PlayStation 1. LCD Soundsystem's *Daft Punk is Playing at My House* will forever remind me of snowboarding in SSX On Tour on the PlayStation 2. The previous version of this game, SSX Tricky, was so named because when your snowboarding character reached a level of points, Run DMC's *Tricky* would play to indicate you had reached "Tricky" status where high level and complex snowboarding maneuvers and tricks could be attempted. This was a powerful and enticing device to draw a user into the game and its goals. This connection between individual "gamer" moments and the songs that accompany them has meant that, gradually, video game music has come to be recognised as equally attendant to the experience of the user and its impact on their experience of immersion and engagement in the gaming environment (Whalen, 2004). Thus musical elements of gaming experiences demonstrate a critical link between immersion in the created game environment and its transition into a "live" experience. This feedback loop between gaming and live music experience occurs both within the game itself and beyond the boundaries of the game and into RL experiences, which emulate and invoke the game experience while adding something new.

Where once game developers created and presented a complete, finished product to an audience who received and consumed the product "as is," gaming is now produced in collaboration. Instructions have even been released so that gamers can create a character in Skyrim that looks like Malukah. This, thanks to her musical rendition of an in-game song "out of world," has led to her RL persona being rendered and recreated within a digital world. The Elder Scrolls Series now comes with a modification-editing tool (mod), to encourage users to create original content to be used by themselves and other gamers. One such "mod" allows a player to patch Malukah's renditions of the Skyrim song into the "in-game" soundtrack. Thus, in the case of Malukah, a live performance and performer have been converted into a digital product, which is then emulated in a live format at a concert, only to be converted back into the digital space of the game.

The transition of digital games from the traditional model of transmitter to receiver has been transformed into a dynamic network of cocreators, who now convert the in-game experience of music into a RL, *live* experience of production and reproduction. Gamers are now able to play the soundtrack of their favored game outside of the realms of the digital space, allowing it to fill the material corporeal world with the remembered experiences of a virtual event. The reciprocal relationship between digital gaming and live music in RL has produced a new and growing community that is born in a virtual space, and rebirthed into the world of the material.

Interactive and immersive features of digital games have transformed the musical landscape into one where gaming culture is generating and reproducing music worthy of aural consumption in its own right. This evolution has resulted in music composed and designed for games forming a legitimate music genre. The sophistication and elegance of these compositions have fully revealed what gamers have known for decades—that gaming is a site for powerful and transformative experiences which are mature, engaging, complex, and most of all, legitimate.

I will never surrender
We'll free the Earth and sky
Crush my heart into embers
And I will reignite ...
I will reignite.

Reignite—*Mass Effect Tribute Song (lyrics by Malukah)*

References

Auslander, P. (2002). Live from cyberspace or, I was sitting at my computer and this guy appeared he thought I was hot. *PAJ: A Journal of Performance and Art*, 24(1), 16–21.

Bennett, L. (2012). Patterns of listening through social media: online fan engagement with the live music experience. *Social Semiotics*, 22(5), 545–557.

BloodReaper (2012). *Skyrim game of the year list. The Elder Scrolls Wiki.* Retrieved from http://elderscrolls.wikia.com/wiki/User_blog:Blood_Reaper/Skyrim_Game_of_the_year_list.

Bordwell, D. & Thompson, K. (1993). *Film art.* New York: McGraw Hill.

Bruns, A. (2008). *Blogs, Wikipedia, Second Life, and beyond: From production to produsage*. Digital Formations (Vol 45). New York, Peter Lang.

Collins, K. (Ed.) (2008). *From Pac-Man to pop music: Interactive audio in games and new media*. Aldershot: Ashgate.

Demers, J. (2006). Dancing machines: 'Dance Dance Revolution', cybernetic dance, and musical taste. *Popular Music*, 25(3), 401–414.

Ellison, N. B. & Boyd, D. (2013). Sociality through social network sites. In W. H. Dutton (Ed.), *The Oxford Handbook of Internet Studies* (pp. 151–172). Oxford: Oxford University Press.

Gamer, P. C. (2012). *Skyrim crowned ultimate game of the year, full list of winners revealed at 30th hmv GamesMaster Golden Joystick Awards. Pc gamer*. Retrieved from http://www.pcgamer.com/2012/10/26/skyrim-crowned-ultimate-game-of-the-year-full-list-of-winners-revealed-at-30th-hmv-gamesmaster-golden-joystick-awards.

Jesper, J. (2005). *Half-real: video games between real rules and fictional worlds*. Cambridge, MA: MIT Press.

King, G. & Krzywinska, T. (2006). *Tomb Raiders and Space Invaders: videogame forms and contexts*. London: I.B. Tauris.

Mark, J. P. & Perron, W. B. (2003). *The video game theory reader*. London: Routledge.

Rheingold, H. (1993). *The virtual community: Homesteading on the electronic frontier*. Cambridge, MA: MIT Press.

Severino, A. (2011). *Game of the year*. PlayStationLifestyle.Net. Retrieved from http://www.playstationlifestyle.net/2011/12/23/game-of-the-year-2011.

Turkle, S. (1997). *Life on the screen: Identity in the age of the Internet*. New York: Simon & Schuster.

Whalen, Z. (2004). Play along—An approach to videogame music. *Games Studies*. Retrieved from http://www.gamestudies.org/0401/whalen.

Section Three

Live after death

Dead music in live music culture

9

F. Cull

In May 2013 at the Old Bar, a small live venue in the northern suburbs of Melbourne, Australia, I saw a magic show and then listened to a banjo player sing songs about the life of an unemployed American during the 1930s. The banjo player, Al Duvall, is from New York, and sings songs that are heavily laced with innuendo, in a style heavily borrowed from the so-called genre Americana.[1] Duvall's press released that he is "a grandchild of the Great Depression… one of the many unemployed musicians in 1932 who was sent via time machine into the future to find work, as part of the WPA [Works Program Administration][2] program" (Duvall, 2013a).

Despite the seemingly antiquated style of music he played, hearing his music in a live environment did not feel strange or alienating. The fact that nobody in the bar appeared old enough to have experienced the Great Depression, and they were even less likely to have experienced it in America, did not matter. We knew the trope and we understood the conventions. We laughed along with the lyrics. It was not so much that we were enjoying the novelty of singing about new problems in an "old-fashioned" style, rather we understood the cultural traditions this music came from and we were enjoying seeing them played out in a new way. We fetishized, repurposed, and performed an on-the-spot auditory analysis, hearing our own issues being performed through an "old-fashioned" lens.

> *I'm picking cotton, I'm picking cotton Over linen, silk or tweed Something simple to go with my old sharecropper shoes And my shares keep going up I've got everything I need Except that lowdown feeling I've got the bluesless blues.*
>
> *From* "Bluesless Blues" *by Al Duvall (2013b)*

[1] According to the Americana Association of America, the genre "Americana" can be defined thus: "American roots music based on the traditions of country. While the musical model can be traced back to the Elvis Presley marriage of 'hillbilly music' and R&B that birthed rock 'n roll, Americana as a radio format developed during the 1990s as a reaction to the highly polished sound that defined the mainstream music of that decade" (see http://americanamusic.org/what-americana, accessed December 23, 2013). As a genre it has also been called alt country or twang core, and it is basically a contemporary genre of music that draws on a number of traditions that have been popular in America since the 1920s, like folk, blues, R&B, rock, and country. Jed Hilly, Executive Director of the Association of Americana Music claims that Bob Dylan admits that he was an Americana artist before it was defined as a genre (see Bloomberg Radio Interview with Jed Hilly, http://americanamusic.org, accessed December 23, 2013). So, it is music that is "classically" American, in a both contemporary and retrospective sense and is now an official musical term and category for the Grammy awards.

[2] The WPA, or Works Progress Administration, was a work relief program run by the American government during the Great Depression; it employed men (and to a lesser extent women) in a variety of roles, some being labor-oriented like building roads and public buildings, but also funding the painting of murals, for example, the restored mural at Cedar Rapids City Hall. The program, headed by an ex-social worker Harry Hopkins, was intended to help the unemployed by "making them useful," rather than paying them a dole payment, which was seen as demoralizing (see Goldberg, 2005).

Duvall's songs are not about the Depression specifically; they merely use the conventions of the genre and our cultural understandings of the time to create meaning. This music could be considered "dead," because it was originally played by artists who long since have died and whose lives bear little similarity to our own—and yet, this music was brought back to life in a live setting.

This chapter explores how this kind of cultural exchange between dead music, new technologies, and live audiences is possible and unpacks the functionalities of it. I question how we connect with music that is not of our own time, how we feel when we hear old tunes on modern listening devices or live in contemporary settings. Simply put, I wonder how digital recordings of music from "another time" interact with our musical present. I consider how fans and musicians consume music in digital archives, and how both groups play a part in the musical reliving of the past. In examining these things, I offer an analysis of the cultural forces that have assisted in bringing "dead" music into "live" music culture, focusing on the impact that the accessibility of digital recordings of music by long dead artists has on our perceptions of live music and also on the live performances of new artists. I do this in four sections.

I commence with an exploration of "deadness" or "dead music" and the meaning of the term within a digital music culture. The fact that digital recordings of music exist means that, for consumers of music culture, time is elastic. For recording artists, death is physical, but it is not auditory. We can still hear songs on the radio from dead recording artists. Mobilizing the work of Stanyek and Piekut, I explore the complexities of the use of the term dead music. I then provide an analysis of one collection in particular, Harry Smith's *Anthology of American Folk Music*, a collection released in 1952 that has gone from obscurity to canon in the last 50 years or so. Here, I am particularly interested in examining how some artists from the musical past get carried forward into the present, while others get forgotten.

In the third section, I further this discussion by unpacking a series of interviews conducted with people involved in the collection and presentation of dead music, including academics, venue owners, radio presenters, and collectors. In these interviews I am not attempting to capture general or international trends; rather, I hope to provide a window into how various people connect to "dead" music to make it "live" for themselves, to see how digital repositories are used—or under-used—by fans of the music they contain, and to find out how different types of music listeners consume digital archives.

Finally, I explore the music of two artists, Al Duvall, who I have already touched on, and Frank Fairfield, an artist who is fetishized for his nostalgic music and style. These artists are contemporary and have released albums in the last two years, but arguably they perform in the style of "dead" music. Auslander suggests that "the idea of liveness is a moving target, a historically contingent concept whose meaning changes over time and is keyed to technology development" (1999, p. xii). These two artists, and their fans and other musical collectors, carry recordings made in the 1920s and 1930s into contemporary live music culture. These artists illuminate ways that we see and experience "dead" music in live culture.

9.1 Deadness in liveness

First, it is important to define what I mean by "dead" and "live," as these terms are not easily given parameters when one is discussing recorded music. Stanyek and Piekut (2010) discuss about ideas of the dead celebrity in relation to the concept of deadness and liveness. They present the argument that deadness, in a culture of recorded and replayed music, takes on myriad complexities and that nobody is truly dead and gone when their voices sing constantly out from the radio, CD player, or television. They also recognized that "the revivification of celebrities has become a key tactic in advertising campaigns for global product lines" (p. 15) and point out that Forbes did a list of the top-earning dead celebrities.[3] This raises questions as to how relevant the concept of mortal death can be in a music culture that is based around digital recordings. When we live in a world where dead performers can take part in live performances, such as through holographic representation, dead and live are no longer solid concepts.[4]

9.1.1 Dead? Music

Stanyek and Piekut clarify that, "as live persons are extended and proliferated through recording technologies and practices, they constantly collaborate with the dead and the not-yet-born" (2010, p. 33). In this way, dead music is a genre that can be poached by musicians who bring the music into live music culture. So, when I talk about "dead" music, I do so in the knowledge that it is not a static concept nor is it a simple one. By "dead" I mean a musical form that evokes the past, either because it was genuinely a part of it or because it imitates and uses elements of the musical form to make meaning.

In the context of a digital music culture, "dead" can mean literal physical death—a musician who is no longer alive. But dead can also mean a musician whose career has gone from producing popular output to no longer charting. Live music now means music played to a live audience, but in the past it also meant musicians who were playing live on radio, until this practice was taken over by radio presenters playing recorded music (Stanyek and Piekut, 2010, p. 28). My focus in this chapter is "dead" music that *sounds* dead, with an awareness that, as Carole Pegg argues, "folk music as a cultural construct, used for a variety of political agendas including nationalism, communism, fascism and colonialism, is the subject of ongoing research and debate" (Pegg, 2001, pp. 63–67). I am not suggesting that the style of music I am focusing on—that is, folky, bluegrass sounds that are based on nostalgic concepts of Americana—is the

[3] They in particular focus on the duet between Natalie Cole and her "dead" father Nat King Cole, "Unforgettable," which was first a song that a "live" Natalie Cole did as a live performance, and then later recorded and released as a single that charted. See Stanyek and Piekut (2010).

[4] Seventeen years after he was shot and killed, a digitally produced hologram of artist Tupac Shakur took part in a live show at Coachella music festival. Although this is an interesting example of digital representations of a dead musician—liveness colliding with deadness—in a live music setting, there are myriad layers to this representation that cannot be covered in this piece, as I wish to focus not on visual representations but instead on the influence of sound (see Harris, 2013).

only genre that plays in and out of these concepts of deadness and liveness. The way in which I am dealing with "deadness" here is that the music that these new artists are mirroring—and these old recordings are of—are considered "dead" and of the past by those that listen to them; they are consumed *because* they feel old and completely removed from the modern world. In the case of an artist like Al Duvall, the contemporary nature of his lyrics is a wink to the true contemporariness of his act, but his music is consumed because the fan wants to connect with the cliché of the "bygone" era. And Frank Fairfield has been referred to as a "time traveler" (Ford, 2015).

9.1.2 Live

The concept of the dead performer in a digital live music culture has significance, because the characteristics of live music are changeable and dependent upon the context in which the performance takes place. They are dependent on a variety of things, not the least of which is the economic infrastructure in which a band or artist attempts to play and the expectations of the fans of that particular music culture. Now that concerts and gigs are digitally recorded, the death of a performer does not remove an artist or their band from live music culture. Through digital technology, we consume digital recordings of live performances and bring them again to "life" and we take part in famous gigs we were not originally a part of and consume their meaning as if we were there.

There are numerous examples of live recordings remaining (or becoming) popular after the death of a musician. Kurt Cobain died in 1994 and yet the MTV Unplugged album has him playing "live" again and again from stereos. And, although Johnny Cash has passed away, his recording of *At Folsom Prison*, recorded in the prison itself, remains part of popular culture. Examples such as this remind us that physical death no longer has the ability to remove the sounds of a band or performer from our day-to-day listening practices. In fact, the death of a musician like Elvis, or even Ian Curtis from Joy Division, becomes central to our popular conception of them; without the interference of new pieces of music, we can bend and manipulate the output the artist made while they were alive into a narrative that suits us. Rather than removing them from popular culture, death, and the consumption of music post-death, transforms and canonizes the artists.[5] As Karja (2006) states, "if history is about choosing those things that are worth telling, then canonization could be described as choosing those things that are worth repeating" (p. 5). Thus, canonization is a process by which "dead" music is strengthened in live music culture.

9.2 Retro-canonization and archivists

A discussion of "dead music"—either antiquated recordings or new artists who are inspired by them—requires considering the process by which certain music was recorded, and therefore remembered, while other music was forgotten. It also requires

[5] See Marcus (1999).

tracking the process by which some recordings become a canon of sorts, while others are seen as unimportant. Albin states that "while digital technology has made it extremely easy to decontextualize musical sounds, to remove them from their original cultural place and moment, it also fosters the possibility that the sounds will attract greater attention and acquire new cultural status" (2002, p. 159). Digital archives, song collectors, and archivists frame understandings of "dead" music. The famous Lomaxes are well known for recording artists like Lead Belly, Burl Ives, and Muddy Waters (Cohen, 2006, p. 54), and British archivists like Frances Child and Cecil Sharp are renowned folk song enthusiasts who collected, archived, and recorded music made by everyday "folk" and by doing so revived and recorded a particular sort of culture for future generations. Without archivists such as these, we would not be able to access "dead" music, but it is important to remember that archiving is not a neutral or objective process.

Archiving is a highly contested process full of moments when certain histories have been obscured in favor of others. Simon Frith (1981) argues that "in the 1930s... song collectors in the US rural South quite often recorded 'authentic' versions of songs learned from the radio a few weeks before" (p. 60). In Harker's (1985) *Fakesong*, he argues that there is a myth-making intent embedded in the work of archivists. Harker states:

> *The problem is that when historians examine the tens of thousands of songs, which appeared in print and were collected by generations of antiquarians, scholars and folklorists, they find that it is very hard to be sure about what, precisely, this evidence represents.*
>
> *(Harker, 1985, p. x)*

So, the collecting of songs must, by its very nature, mean that parts of musical history are forgotten or assumed. By this logic, the strict definitions of what is authentic music—specifically folk in these cases—and what it is not is a process of privileging some parts of history while forgetting others. As Frith echoes: "the ideology of folk that was developed at the end of the nineteenth century reflected not existing musical practices, but a nostalgia for how they might have been" (1981, p. 159). This means that there is a political impetus behind the work of music archivists, one of myth-making and a construction of an idealized past and a nation-state. This should not be a minor consideration when thinking about our present understandings of archives, as engagement with "dead" music is often based on a nostalgic idea of the past as represented by constructed archives. Contemporary consumption of digital recordings of "dead" music shows a desire for authenticity, which may indeed be a search for something that never really existed and, surely, for something that has been constructed after the fact.

The process of canonization of certain collections is a consequence of some recordings being lauded for their authenticity. The process of canonization is central to the processes of how this "antiquated" music style remains present in live music culture. Canonization is complex and in some cases the elevation of one type of music or collection over another seems accidental, or at least a combination of factors that seem serendipitous. This is particularly true of the *Anthology of American Folk Music*. The *Anthology* was released in 1952. It was a three-volume LP collection that was curated by Harry Smith. Moses Asch, the founder of Folkways Records, met Smith and asked him to assemble an anthology from his massive record collection. The records he included spanned 1920 to 1930—rare recordings that he had collected during World War II (Skinner, 2006, p. 69). In 1997, Smith's *Anthology of American Folk Music* was reissued as a six-CD box set and subsequently won Grammies for Best Historical Album and Best Album Notes (Rosenberg, 1998, p. 327).

In Skinner's work on the *Anthology*, " 'Must be Born Again': resurrecting the *Anthology of American Folk Music*", Skinner demonstrates that, in the case of the Harry Smith collection, we can see that the process of how dead music is collected, listened to, and popularized is trackable, but not predictable. Listeners remember what they want, when they want to, rather than recalling exactly how things "really" were. Skinner shows that in the 45 years between the original release and the reissue that its reputation and significance morphed and it became part of a canon amongst collectors and musicians alike (2006, pp. 57–61). Since, the collection has become so celebrated, one might assume that there was at least a moderate level of popularity and celebration at the time of its initial release. On the contrary, Skinner found that the first mention of the collection by any journalist was a "throw away" comment in *Sing Out*! in 1952. And in academia, the first acknowledgement of the collection as influential was in 1977 (2006, p. 61). Skinner argues:

> *The scarcity of articles that mention the Anthology suggests that prior to its re-issue, most journalists and critics did not consider the Anthology to be the major conduit for the folk revival.*
>
> *(Skinner, 2006, p. 62)*

And yet, by the early 1990s, the *Anthology* was considered central.

So what are the cultural processes at play here? Skinner clarifies:

> *No single factor was responsible or the Anthology's elevated status—including the reputations of Asch and Smith,[6] the form and content of the release, the cultural legitimacy offered by its Smithsonian tag[7] or the rise of the new genre of "Americana" music.*
>
> *(Skinner, 2006, p. 71)*

Before considering the form and content of the release, the digital aspects of the collection and how they may have contributed to the change in reception from the 1960s to the 1990s need to be discussed. In the 1960s, books and broadsides used to be the norm and "collections of documents from popular and vernacular culture were

[6] Smith was an artist who was associated with Allen Ginsberg and the Chelsea Hotel, which lends him a pop culture authenticity that's hard to shake (Skinner, 2006; Rosenberg, 1998).

[7] Asch intended the *Folkways* collection to be marketed towards libraries and museums, which means that the *Anthology* ended up in "legitimate" cultural repositories, which helps it be represented as "high" culture (see Skinner, 2006).

published in books as folk song" (Rosenberg, 1998, p. 329). However, Skinner quotes Bob Dylan arguing that "those records were around—that Harry Smith anthology—but that's not what everybody was listening to... mostly you heard other performers... you could hear the *actual* people singing those ballads" (2006, p. 64). Dylan further argued that most people in the "scene" were transient and therefore would not have owned the record or a record player (2006, p. 64). Additionally, Rosenberg states that the collection "cost nearly thirty-five dollars at a time when most albums sold for three or four dollars" (1998, p. 328) so affordability was an issue. This of course changed in the 1990s, when the *Anthology* was reissued. CDs were more affordable and by the 1990s most people would have owned a CD player.

Smith organized the content of his *Anthology* to align with emerging liberal politics. Many of the music collections up until this period were racially segregated and the collections of the time can reveal much about race relations. Skinner shows that at the time, white musicians' recordings were grouped together and black musicians' recordings were grouped together. White working-class, rural musicians were called "hillbillies" and black musicians' songs were "race" songs and all others were labeled as "ethnic" (Skinner, 2006, pp. 63–65). Instead of following this pattern, Smith's categories were "Ballads," "Social Music," and "Songs"—so sound and content were the way the songs were defined (2006, p. 65). Collections like Smith's allow us to view our past in a more acceptable way, because *Anthology* was not marked by race. In this way, retro-canonization and the editing of archivists impacts our views of the musical past. People liked the view that Smith presented, and so his collection has become a valuable collection of "dead" music, for both collectors and musicians.

9.3 Collector interviews

Wanting to look more deeply into the revival of dead music in contemporary culture, at a local and individual level, I interviewed a small cross section of "dead" music enthusiasts in Melbourne. They were Joel Morrison, a booking agent for pub venues; Suzi Lanagan, a community radio presenter for the show "What the Folk" on PBS.FM 106.7; music psychologist, Dr Tim Byron; lecturer and student of traditional Irish song, Narelle McCoy; "record geek" and music student, John Encarnacao; and a self-described "listener," Brian Vincent. I first asked them whether or not they would describe themselves as collectors. All respondents agreed that yes, they were music collectors, in a variety of formats—Tim: "CDs and vinyl"; Narelle: "Any format"; John: "CDs, digital, and vinyl"; Susi: "CDs and digital"; Joel: "Mostly vinyl but anything will do"; and Brian: "Vinyl or CD."

To define oneself as a collector has a variety of connotations. A collector is a music consumer who engages with music beyond casual listening. They are someone who seeks to own and acquire the music they enjoy and become a curator of sorts, either in terms of collecting a particular genre or in amassing a large library. Collecting habits are thus an active and evolving process of engaging with music culture. I asked the interviewees to go into more detail about the type of listener they felt they were.

Tim: I am a very broad listener, who wants to know everything about every sort of music.
Narelle: I love the experience of a wide and diverse range of music. Anything from Hildegard of Bingem to Tupac and beyond! As for folk and world music, I am open to new sounds and old favorites. My main focus is Irish traditional but it is not the entirety of my listening scope. I'm also fascinated by the blending of old and modern, which has given rise to the misnomer "world music."
John: I listen to music every day, although I am not someone that has music on all the time… I always need to have music that is new to me around, regardless of how old it is. I feel it is important to listen to at least some music that is being produced in the present, even though I have no illusions of "keeping up" with stuff. … variety is really important to me in my listening habits—jazz, art music, pop songs, and particularly music on the experimental fringes of pop and rock. If I had the time, I could pretty much make mix CDs and compilations of certain artists' work almost incessantly.
Susi: As a radio presenter of a world folk music show, I'm obviously a very keen collector with the added enjoyment of choosing tracks that I think my listeners would like too.
Joel: Definitely defines the greater part of my life.
Brian: I would like to think that I don't obsess; I am a "serious" listener in that I can't use music as something to simply kill silence. I listen to most of my music alone and always have done. However, I do enjoy listening to music with others who can appreciate it. I do want to listen to as many types of music as I can. However I have to enjoy the music in some way or another, it doesn't have to sound pleasant or "catchy" but it's essential that I sense some form of integrity in the music. This said I cannot listen to music with lyrics I strongly disagree with; the content of the song becomes too much of an obstacle for me to continue listening. This is also true if a singer has a tone of voice or style of singing I find weak, without novelty or uncharismatic.

I also asked how they feel about music that could be described as "old" or "antiquated." I did not give them parameters of what old or antiquated music meant, as I did not want to limit their responses—I wanted to know their response to "dead" music, as they themselves would define it.

Tim: Sometimes it can be spooky, like you're listening to the past; e.g. if I listen to Robert Johnson, it sounds somehow unearthly.
Narelle: I love the notion of hearing an interpretation of a song from a revered singer who has left their personal ornamentation for others to appreciate. … It carries the tradition forward and gives the notion of continuity. It also inspires me to experiment with my own technique.
John: There is a particular sense of remove, or wonder, at listening to pre-WWII music, I feel. The Harry Smith anthology, Bessie Smith, Robert Johnson ….
Joel: Listening to some of the really old blues recordings of people like Mississippi John Hurt, Robert Johnson, Geechie Wiley, Leadbelly, etc. raise some pretty dark and grim spectres. The music sounds so plaintive and raw.
Brian: At its best, it touches me to the very core of my being and I feel one with humanity. Though they are important, it's not just the singer, the song or the music, it's those moments in the history of human experience captured, I think this is the essence of folk music. With old folk recordings, the person performing is not an artist in the conventional sense, they may be a factory worker or a farm laborer, so what one is listening to is the only chance this person may get to really express themselves. This is a very special thing. I particularly like field recordings as often you can hear the creak or squeak of an instrument's keys or the chair the performer may sitting on, it instills a rawness and aura of authenticity to the recording.

Here all the interviewees spoke of the music and their reaction to it with awareness of the "deadness" of the old music they enjoyed. The experience of listening to recordings of artists that are long dead is done so with a connection to the artists as if they are ghosts, but the engagement is with "deadness" is made possible through digital mediation. The fact that the artists are dead is part of the enjoyment—it is also part of the authenticity that the interviewees enjoyed. It's the "liveness" of the digital recording combined with the "deadness" of the subject that produces an emotional reaction in the listener.

Since all interviewed subjects had defined themselves as active collectors of "dead" music, I asked them about their engagement with archives, like the Library of Congress' Lomax collection. The answers here challenged my assumptions, as I had thought that anyone with an interest, academic or otherwise, in antiquated music would engage with these repositories frequently. However, when I asked them if they had ever accessed any archive available to them, their responses were inconsistent.

Tim: Yes—most often the live music archive at archive.org.
Narelle: Yes from the Lomax collection, the Smithsonian, the Irish Traditional Music Archive, the National Folklore Collection at the University College in Dublin.
John: Rarely if ever.
Susi: Rarely, but have used the Lomax collection.
Joel: I'll pick up the records of Folkways and Lomax if I find them, but mostly I get stuff through recommendations or something I'd read about.
Brian: No, I have only purchased albums from the Smithsonian Folkways website.

Only Tim and Narelle, the academics working in musical fields, engaged with archives in intimate depth. Others had limited experience, but, overall, enthusiasm for the collections was not strong. It appeared that music collectors without a direct academic motivation assumed that the archives were not for them because they are not pitched to fans. I later tested this thesis with the collectors, asking them if they thought of archives as a purely academic resource:

Tim: I have accessed them for academic purposes, but I do access them because I enjoy listening to the music. I'm sure that music archives only being accessed for academic or research purposes is partly a consequence of copyright law. The only music which is legally in a bunch of archives is long out of copyright, and thus often of poor recording quality.
Narelle: As a singer, I was interested in Irish songs from the woman's perspective. This was initially for performance but led me to the research I'm currently pursuing for my PhD.
John: I don't know… I would think it a positive thing if people who were not engaged in research were encouraged to use archives such as these.
Susi: I just don't really use it. However, I reap the benefit when I play musicians who have researched songs and music for me to play.
Joel: Archives just don't really apply to me.
Brian: I don't know that much about them, I do think more people should be aware of these archives and have access to them.

There is an intriguing disconnection between the fans of the music and their accessing of their original repositories. As John points out, although "it's a positive thing" for people to engage with archives, it seems as if they are an untapped resource for everyday collectors of the genre.

It is particularly interesting that Tim felt that the recordings were of poor quality and therefore something he did not often access. This is in direct opposition to Brian's almost fetishist desire to hear background noise, etc., the hallmarks of a poor recording—but Brian's experience of these recordings largely comes from vinyl or CD. The authenticity and the emotions brought forward by this are attached to the format. Most respondents have used the digital archives, but they seem to view them with less enthusiasm as their physical music collections. In the interviews, it seemed that the digital archives were not seen as the catalyst for the resurrection of the dead music, but, rather, a cemetery for people to metaphorically "read the headstones" and decide which graves to "dig up"—for research, performance, or personal interest purposes.

Digital archives allow unprecedented access to "dead" music. However, the exchange between listener and the music is complex. Here it appears that the digitization of dead music archives reaffirms the authenticity of non-digital musical forms, "old-fashioned" artists and the authenticity already associated with "folk" musical forms. However, to bring the music to life and to affirm its authenticity, my interviewees suggest that often a "better" and more authentic non-digital version of the music will be sought.

9.4 Frank Fairfield—time traveler

The digitization of dead music archives reaffirms the authenticity of non-digital musical forms, and "old-fashioned" artists, as well as the authenticity already associated with "folk" musical forms. However, another step in this process is the desire to see and hear "dead" music re-performed in a live setting. Retro-canonization of dead music archives, influences "live" music culture, in that performers, presenters, and venue owners encourage the process of these sounds and musical forms being played, adopted by new artists, and then heard by new audiences (Auslander, 1999).

This complex interplay between digital archives and "dead" music informs a unique version of live music in the present. My examination of the musician Frank Fairfield demonstrates this final step in the resurrection of "dead" music. Fairfield is not an old musician—He was born in 1986 and became a musician in his twenties—and yet he plays music that would not sound out of place on the *Anthology of American Folk Music*. Marcus describes Fairfield as:

> *A young Californian who sings and plays as someone who's crawled out of the Virginia mountains carrying familiar songs that in his sound forgotten: broken lines, a dissonant drone, the fiddle or the banjo all percussion, every rising moment louder than the one before it.*
>
> *Weiss (2009)*

I saw Frank Fairfield at the Meredith Music Festival in 2011. I stood in a natural amphitheater in modern-day Australia and my filthy boots were no longer filthy because I was at a music festival. Once he started playing, the dust up my nose was not from various delinquent university students, expensively shod feet, instead I was transported to the Dust Bowl in Oklahoma. The feelings I got while listening to Fairfield's music were not like the ghostly apparitions that my interviewees who listened to recordings spoke of, they were visceral. The music was not dead anymore, it had come to life. In the *LA Weekly*, Weiss wrote:

> *The question lingers: why should you listen to an ostensibly callow kid whose junior high years paralleled the boy band era, when each year, the amount of high quality archival music multiplies exponentially—to say nothing of the treasures Alan Lomax unearthed.*
>
> *Weiss (2013)*

I argue that people listen to this music in new artists like Frank Fairfield because they want experiences like mine: a connection to the past in the "here and now." For Fairfield, this desire is not necessarily apparent. He wonders, "why would anyone listen to me when you can hear Uncle Dave Macon or Wilmer Watts?" (Weiss, 2013). Yet, Fairfield's fans, who may want to consume the digital archives of music from the past, want to see the "dead" music they love performed in a live context too. In this way, digital music archives, which allow us to hear songs like "Darlin' Cory" and understand their history, connects with a live music culture.

What interests me regarding Frank Fairfield is that he represents a musical past in his sound, but does not acknowledge this—he in fact disagrees with this idea of a musical past. He is often depicted as a time traveler, but he himself claims that the folk songs he plays are actually the only popular music and that they therefore are about now. In a documentary on Fairfield by More Dust Than Digital, he is pictured collecting old 78s. Asked about how he feels about pop music, Fairfield states, "There is no popular music these days, there's corporate music" (Weiss, 2013). Fairfield then does a performance of the folk song "Darlin' Cory." Darlin' Cory is a song that was first collected by Cecil Sharp from the Appalachian Mountains in 1918. The first known recording of the song is from 1927 (Matteson, 2013; Smithsonian Folkways, 2014). Speaking about "Darlin' Cory," he explains his feelings about the idea that he and the song are from the past:

> *This is popular music. These are popular songs. Darlin' Cory is a popular song; that song has been sung millions of times. That's what I really love about these songs. You know... I don't think they're old songs. They're here. They're now songs. They're songs that people sing. All there is is here, now. This is what music is. Nothing begins. Nothing ends. It's the way it is.*
>
> *Wilson (2013)*

I argue that Fairfield's perception of time is central to how music that sounds like his comes through to live music culture. His belief in the idea that folk music is the only popular music is not unique, but I find his idea that the nostalgia that the sound of the music is so associated with is misplaced very interesting. He denies the idea that this music is "old" at all and brings the folk traditions of singing old songs nobody remembers who wrote into contemporary digital music culture with his albums.

9.4.1 Conclusion

Digital archives, despite the fact that the collecting process is indeed biased, remain an untapped resource full of songs like "Darlin' Cory" that may have been pushed aside but could be unearthed as collectors and musicians dig through the graveyard of dead music. Through this exploration, I argued that dead music is ultimately an elastic term with multiple definitions, as the physical death of an artist who has been recorded is not the death of their music. Instead, "dead" music is a term that suits a particular sound, rather than a reference to music made be dead artists.

When asked if people are wrong to think his music represents a trip to the past, Frank Fairfield said:

> *You know, people talking about the past, it's all the same stuff right here all the time... You know, I want to continue playing the music that people used to play before it got cast aside.*
>
> *Gonyea (2010)*

For Fairfield, this music is not dead. And in a strange relationship, digital recordings of music have meant that artists from the past, the dead, live in our culture now. The complex relationship between digital archives, "dead" music enthusiasts, and the persistent desire to enjoy music in a live setting has influenced contemporary artists, like Fairfield, to produce a sound that is reminiscent of "dead" music, and in this way, the music has become part of live music culture again.

Acknowledgments

I'd like to thank all my interviewees for taking part in the research for this chapter. I would also like to thank Dan for the initial conversations that sparked the idea for it.

References

Auslander, P. (1999). *Liveness: Performance in mediatized culture*. London: Routledge.

Cohen, R. (2006). *Folk Music: The Basics* (Routledge edition).

Duvall, A. (2013a). *Bluesless blues' from squirt, rubber heart 2011*. Retrieved from http://alduvall.bandcamp.com.

Duvall, A. (2013b). *Melbourne—The music network events*. Retrieved from http://events.themusicnetwork.com/2013/al-duvall/melbourne/fitzroy.

Ford, J. (2015). A look back at some of Charlottsville's musical highs. http://www.c-ville.com/a-look-back-at-some-of-charlottsvilles-musical-highs/#.VXV_gUYWNYI. Accessed 08/06/2015.

Frith, S. (1981). "The magic that can set you free": The ideology of folk and the myth of the rock community. In R. Middleton & D. Horn (Eds.), *Popular music; Folk or popular? Distinctions, influences, continuities*. Cambridge: Cambridge University Press.

Gonyea, D. (2010). *Frank Fairfield: A one man folk revival*. National Public Radio. http://www.wbur.org/npr/128823639, 23 Dec. 2014.

Harker, D. (1985). *Fakesong—the manufacture of British "folksong" 1700 to the present day*. Milton Keynes and Philadelphia: Open University Press.

Harris, M. (2013). The hologram of Tupac at Coachella and saints: The value of relics for devotees. *Celebrity Studies*, 4(2), 238–240.

Karja, A. (2006). A prescribed alternative mainstream: Popular music and canon formation. *Popular Music*, 25(1), 3–19.

Marcus, G. (1999). *Dead Elvis: A chronicle of a cultural obsession*. London: Harvard University Press.

Matteson, R. (2013). *Darling Corey: History' bluegrass series. Matteson art*. Retrieved from http://www.mattesonart.com/darlin-corey-history.aspx.

Pegg, C. (2001). Folk music. In S. Sadie & J. Tyrrell (Eds), *The New Grove Dictionary of Music and Musicians*. Oxford: Oxford University Press.

Rosenberg, N. (1998). Anthology of American Folk Music and working class music. *Labour*, 42, 327–332.

Skinner, K. (2006). Must be born again: Resurrecting the anthology of American Folk Music. *Popular Music*, 25(1), 57–75.

Smithsonian Folkways (2014). *'Darling Corey' archives*. Smithsonian Folkways. Retrieved from http://www.folkways.si.edu/search?JsonSearchModel={%22FiltersModel%22%3A{%22AppliedFilters%22%3A{}%2C%22AvailableContentTypes%22%3A[]%2C%22ContentType%22%3A0}%2C%22PaginationModel%22%3A{%22ResultsPerPage%22%3A20%2C%22StartItemIndex%22%3A0}%2C%22Query%22%3A%22Cora%22%2C%22SelectedView%22%3A0%2C%22SortingOption%22%3A0%2C%22SpellingSuggestionSearchRestricted%22%3Afalse}&query=darling%20corey.

Stanyek, J. & Piekut, B. (2010). Deadness: Technologies of the intermundane. *The Drama Review*, 54(1), 14–38.

Weiss, J. (2009). *Frank Fairfield: The man who wasn't there*. LA Weekly. Retrieved from http://www.laweekly.com/2009-10-15/music/frank-fairfield-the-man-who-wasn-39-t-there.

Wilson, A. (2013). *Frank Fairfield documentary. More dust than digital productions*. Retrieved from http://vimeo.com/9660443.

Goldberg, C. A. (2005). Contesting the status of relief workers during the New Deal. The workers alliance of America and the works progress administration, 1935–1941. *Social Science History*, 29(3), 337–371.

Keepin' it real? Life, death, and holograms on the live music stage

10

A. Jones, R. Bennett, and S. Cross

10.1 Introduction

Definitions of live music and "live" performance have expanded to accept digital screens, sounds, manipulations, interventions—and even musicians—as valid parts of a live concert. Today electronic instruments, voice-altering technologies, screen projections, and sampling software are taken for granted aspects of the *mise en scène* of the live music stage. As audiences and performers become comfortable interacting in virtual worlds and with digital conventions, the boundaries for "live" performance are shifting not only to include DJs who play digital samples in real-time for a large audiences but also virtual performers like UK band, the Gorillaz, who headlined Glastonbury in 2010, without any human bodies on stage.

In the case of the Gorillaz, the virtual band on stage refers to a group of actual musicians—Damon Albarn, Jaime Hewlett, and various recognizable corporeal music artists. While the virtual characters are not intended to refer to single musicians per se, their collective representation acts as an avatar for a presumably real-life band, with flesh-and-blood referents. The audience's willingness to accept Gorillaz' virtual stage-presence indicates a social acceptance of digital manifestations of a real-life band. However, this chapter is interested in the virtual holographic humanoid forms on the live music stage where it is difficult to connect the virtual performers to actual "live" bodies. It explores themes of liveness and presence in a comparison of two live music holograms: the Tupac hologram (also known as "Pac-O-Gram" (Spencer-Hall, 2012, pp. 56–71), who "appeared" onstage with Snoop Dog and Dr. Dre at Coachella in 2012 after the "real" rapper's death in 2006, and the live concerts headlined by the humanoid Anime J-Pop[1] star Hatsune Miku.

Analysis of online fan comments, popular press, blogs, opinion pieces, and academic papers regarding both Hatsune Miku and the Tupac hologram, raises ontological and ethical questions concerning the future of the hologram on the live music stage. It will be argued that while the hologram is *already* an acceptable presence on the live music stage, genre conventions, performance narratives, and ontological and ethical conditions—especially regarding transparency of the technological and artificial construction of the artist; whether the hologram appears to resurrect a dead body or create a new body; and whether who owns and profits from the holographic form is clearly defined—impact on spectator willingness to accept the presence itself as "live."

[1] J-Pop is an abbreviation of Japanese Popular Music.

The Digital Evolution of Live Music

10.2 Presence

The creation of presence through technology is not a new phenomenon. Since the advent of the telegraph in the 1840s, there has been a perceived connection between communication technology and the creation of otherworldly presence. Dissolving the barriers between time and space, communication technology was able to make "what is not present, present" (Zhao, 2003, p. 144). Similarly, Sconce explores the notion of presence created within electronic media where the technology appears to be imbued with a sense of "liveness" and voices inhabit the technology with an eerie electronic presence (Sconce, 2000, pp. 17–18). Within its wires and fibers, communication technology holds a history of presence: the telegraph delivered messages, the telephone was inhabited by voices, self-contained worlds could be found inside the television, and the Internet allows users to create a version of themselves to engage with a multitude of virtual spaces. While Sconce's work explores the creation of presence where the technology is seen as a "gateway into a self-sustaining and wholly enclosed electronic elsewhere" (Sconce, 2000, pp. 17–18), the recent emergence of the hologram sees this presence escape the bounds of the technology and take its place on the live stage alongside physical musicians.

Since the appearance of the Tupac hologram at Coachella in 2012, there has been much discussion surrounding the technical aspects of holograms; many have disputed using the term "hologram" to describe the presence on the stage, as the image projections commonly used on stage are technically not holograms as often depicted within science fiction popular culture. They are instead a play on an old magician's trick, Pepper's Ghost (Nickell, 2005, p. 288), which makes the 3D projection appear as though it is a hologram. In this chapter the intention is not to discuss the technology used to create the hologram or redefine the term; instead the focus is on the ontological impact on the audience. Therefore, Spensor-Hall's definition will be utilized. The hologram is described as "the spectral appearance of (computerised) bodies through unobtrusive or overtly unacknowledged artificial means" (Spencer-Hall, 2012, p. 57), or where the holograms appears on the stage alongside other live musicians, unhindered, where the presence of the technology is invisible to the audience.

In order for the audience to accept the hologram as a legitimate presence upon the stage, it must appear to be as authentic as a corporeal musician that inhabits the stage. There must be the feeling of co-presence, where each artist becomes "accessible, available and subject to one another" (Goffman, 1963, p. 22). Known as *Impression Management*, an individual must maintain the impression of the self in order to maintain and display the authentic self to others. Goffman asserts that the authenticity of this performance is determined by the signs that we "give or give off" (Goffman, 1959, p. 14) in the presence of others. When considering live performance, if the holographic presence created upon the stage does not "give off" the appropriate indications of the artist's self, then the authenticity of its presence is brought into question. The Gorillaz performance at the 2007 MTV awards hologram is an example. The cartoon characters are not reproductions of living people; however, as holograms, there is still the need to legitimize their presence upon the stage and prove a sense of liveness on the stage in order for the audience to accept the hologram's authentic presence. This was illustrated by the insertion of the corporeal Madonna into the performance. Madonna, through the presence of her physical form interacting with, walking behind, and singing to the holographic musicians gave the performance a live edge and legitimacy as a live act. Her physical presence allowed the technology to become invisible and furthered the illusion of the Gorillaz being there live on the stage.

If the technology used to create the presence becomes too visible to the audience, their ability to suspend their disbelief is broken and the authenticity of the presence upon the stage comes into question. "These negotiations between artist and audience surrounding technological tools and the resultant effects on expectation, immersion and participation in performance are likely to be rewarding and challenging for both parties" (Bennett, 2012, p. 554). This is especially important when applied to the live audience's acceptance of the holographic presence as an authentic representation of the dead star. In the case of the Gorillaz, there is no need to legitimize the "realness" of the hologram, as they never have corporeally existed. The following sections explore such issues of presence and authenticity, with a focus on genre, ontology, and ethics when the hologram is the reproduction of a recently deceased person such as the Tupac hologram, or when the hologram is created such as Hatsune Miku.

10.3 Genre

10.3.1 Pac-o-gram and hip-hop

Tupac Shakur, alternatively known as 2pac, came to fame in the early 1990s. He began his career as a backup rapper and dancer for Digital Underground and released his first album in 1991 *2Pacalypse Now* to mixed reviews. Throughout the early 1990s, until his death by shooting in 1996, he released six albums. A further eight Tupac albums have been released posthumously. Tupac's lyrics were infused with his social and political views and he was touted by *Rolling Stone* (2014) as one of the most influential rappers of all time. So when his hologram appeared on stage at Coachella music festival alongside rap royalty Dr. Dre and Snoop Dog, it caused a mixed reaction from the hip-hop community.

A life-size Tupac appeared on the Coachella stage wearing white baggy pants, a gold belt, gold chain with crucifix and signature Timberland boots (Westfesttv, 2012). The image of the Pac-o-gram was true to the artist's hip-hop aesthetic. He stood on stage, shirtless-arms outstretched, put his mike to his mouth, and yelled, "What up Coachella" to the audience, before launching into his performance of "Hail Mary" (Kaufman, 2012). The resurrected image of Tupac as a hologram has religious undertones. From the Jesus-like stance, to Tupac's swinging crucifix, and the choice of "Hail Mary" as the song, there is a push towards the performance as a resurrection, with the desire to bring Tupac "back to life" (Kaufman, 2012). However, the light on the edge of the choreographed Pac-o-gram, the points where you can see through the body, and finally his disappearance into a flash of light suggest that this performer was less a resurrection and more the presence of a ghost on stage. The Pac-o-gram switches between delivering a performance of the "real" Tupac (in his aesthetics, voice, and song); the artificiality of holographic form (in the translucency, glitches in the image and repetitive movement) and the producers' construction (in the address to the audience, song choice and choreography). The inconsistencies in *Impression Management* failed to remove the presence of the technology and, consequently, the hip-hop community critiqued the authentic presence of Tupac within this performance.

Keeping it real and a connection to roots (both ethnically and musically) underpin the hip-hop genre, and the Pac-o-gram "resurrection" challenged this foundation. The source of authenticity for hip=hop artists has historically been noted as staying true to origin, identification with ethnicity—traditionally blackness, but in contemporary hip-hop whiteness too, "not selling out" and being "hard" (Fraley, 2009, p. 42; Forman, 2000; Armstrong, 2004). Rapping and the image of the hip-hop artist is both a process of expressing and sustaining a "real" identity. The "realness" of the Pac-o-gram as staying true to both Tupac's image and ideology (this will be discussed later in the chapter) is questionable. Aesthetically the Pac-o-gram, tattooed and clothed, stayed true to the "look" of Tupac. "Ultimately, hip hop authenticity requires that artists stay true to one's self in matters of thinking and being" (Fraley, 2009, p. 42). This "realness" and "authenticity" of the rap artist gained more cultural currency as hip-hop gained popularity in the 1980s and became mainstream in the 2000s. Tupac as a rap icon in the 1990s was idolized for being true to "the game" (of life), but the Pac-o-gram has removed this ability from him. The subject of being "legit[imate]" heavily dominated the lyrics of popular artists, including Tupac, during the movement to a mainstream genre. So too do stories about remembering the rapper's origins, the drug-addled lives led, prison time, as well as crime and death on the streets. While Dre and Snoop are legitimated by the hip-hop culture as authentic rap artists, through their creation of the Pac-o-gram, they have created an inauthentic piece of rap culture, stripping something real of its roots and soul. For hip-hop artists the notion of authenticity and keepin' it real has, as Fraley and Jones (2006) suggest, emerged as "a node through which flows arguments about who's capable, or not, of legitimately interpreting a culture, and therefore, participating in its most esoteric forms of antecedent oral and aesthetic culture …" (Fraley, 2009, p. 42). This is recognized through the long-standing debate over whether white men and women can rap. The controversy over the white Australian female rapper Iggy Azalea is the most contemporary example of this. This need for an unwavering connection between artist, art, and origins, while a defining characteristic of the genre, is not necessarily unique to hip-hop; however, alternative genres do not carry with them such strict rules for content and performance.

10.3.2 Hatsune Miku and J-Pop

Hatsune Miku is a humanoid vocaloid performer created by Crypton Future Music; translated into English, her name means "first sound from the future" (Crypton Future Media, 2014). She was developed using the Yamaha vocaloid software and samples from voice actress Saki Fugita, and anime/manga artist Kei Garō designed the image of Hatsune Miku: a female who is perpetually 16 years of age, 158 cm tall, 42 kg, and a Virgo (Crypton Future Media, 2014). The color of turquoise hair, and trim on her skirt, boots, arm-warmers, and nails, can be linked to the signature color of the Yamaha software, and the patterns on her boots, skirt and arm-warmers look similar to musical bars on the synthesizer software. Miku is drawn as an attractive female anime teenager, and resembles other Japanese pop culture images of females such as Sailor Moon. Since the first release of the software in 2007 Hatsune has been performing sold-out 3D concerts worldwide. By 2014, she had released 100,000 songs, and amassed 900,000 Facebook fans (Crypton Future Media, 2014). Hatsune is not just an animated software program, she is a digital diva who has gained global notoriety as a live performer.

The live performance presents Hatsune as a three-dimensional hologram backed by a live non-holographic band. In her live performances, Hatsune is dressed in her signature outfit, in which she dances and sings a range of songs, which have been created by those producers who have purchased the software. While the image stays true to her digital persona, her movement, while at times pixilated, has been choreographed to appear humanlike. She bops, twirls, and windmills her arms like a rockstar, moving around the stage as the audience encourages the performance. The hologram has been created to give "life" to the virtual popstar.

Like non-digital "live" performers, Miku performs up to three-hour concerts and her performances are complete with lightshows and backup dancers. She also occasionally performs with other holographic performers, and in 2014 was the opening act for Lady Gaga's Artpop Ball (JiJi, 2014). In dual holographic performances, the holograms are choreographed so that they go either in front or behind each other, to give the illusion that they are dancing together. Similar to the Tupac hologram, the pixilation of the performer, glitches in lighting, and limitation of the movement (especially during dual holographic performances) remind the viewer that this is a hologram. While the visibility of the technology reminds the audience that this is a digital representation of the flesh and blood of Tupac, for Hatsune, this is true to her "digital" self. She was born of technology and the hologram is the "live" version of this digital image. To dress a human as Hatsune would strip the authenticity from the performance. The realness of Hatsune comes from her as a digital creation, a mashup of anime looks, synth vocals, J-pop tunes, and human movement, which her fans, producers and the software company have all helped to create. This also stays true to the sub-genre of Japanese popular music that Hatsune is situated in.

The J-Pop—Japanese popular music—genre, in stark contrast to hip-hop, is recognized for its cultural appropriations and mish-mash of "inter-ethnic" (Moody, 2006, p. 220) language, and aesthetics. From the 1960s to the 1990s it was known for its Beatlish influences (boy bands, catchy lyrics, and riffs); Hosokawa (1999) writes that this genre "tends to be heavily influenced by Western styles but mixed with something Japanese in the lyrics, rhythm, melody and/or arrangement. (Japanese lyrics are particularly crucial for nationwide popularity)" (p. 519). In the 1990s, J-Pop diversified with the additions of J-hip-hop and urban pop, and in the 2000s, anime vocaloid music. This is recognized in not only the mashup of musical styles and aesthetics that underpin Hatsune's image as a performer, but also the numerous contributors to her live performance, as well as her growing discography, developed using the synthesizer software. Effectively, anyone who has a computer can create J-popstars like Hatsune using the software and song actresses. The vocaloid/anime genre is now, globally, one of the most recognized and popular forms of J-Pop (Conner, 2013).

10.4 Ontology

A hologram on the live music stage, whether animated or resurrected, raises ontological questions regarding the nature of the legitimacy of its "being." This is especially true in the case of Pac-o-gram and Hatsune, as there is not a live body to connect the holographic image to. Pandelakis links this ontological dilemma to the "potential reality of the hologram, and the ways in which it questions our own identity as a subject." If a hologram becomes "too real" and its ability to project, reproduce or contain a human "self" that looks *life-like* causes an "eerie" response in many people, that Japanese robot designer Mori Masahiro calls the "uncanny valley." Masahiro found that people were very willing to develop an affinity for robots that demonstrated human behaviors and which had characteristics and bodies similar to people. However, when the robots began to appear too close to human, so much so that they could "almost" be mistaken for one, the affinity towards the robot disappeared and turned into feelings of fear, revulsion, and unease.

The ontological themes found in fan responses to both YouTube videos of the holographic artists, and in comments to online news and blog stories, places the Tupac hologram in the uncanny valley category for many, as using holographic technology to resurrect a dead artist sits uncomfortably with audiences. Alternatively, the Hatsune hologram—which never had a "real" body in the first place—is able to form a deep affinity amongst her fans, perhaps due to the fact that the hologram does not claim to replace or resurrect an actual human in any way. Form an ontological perspective, it seems that in the case of these two holographic performers, audiences are more comfortable with bodies that emerge from the simulacra and are *brought to life*, rather than actual human bodies that are brought *back* to life.

10.4.1 Pac-o-gram

Much of the discussion and controversy surrounding the Tupac hologram did not lie in the use of technology to create a holographic presence on stage, but in the uncomfortable space between life and death where the image is situated. A resurrection narrative was apparent in the Coachella performance, as there was no "tribute," forewarning, or introduction to the entrance of the hologram that hinted at its artificiality. Rather, an image of Tupac just "appeared" on the stage and addressed the audience, even though the original Tupac had never performed there. The narrative and the holographic image itself aimed to make "Pac-o-gram" appear as close to the original Tupac as possible. On stage, Pac-o-gram was treated as a "guest" artist, joining the performance for a couple of songs, similar to the appearance of the actual body of rapper Eminem, later in the set.

The presence of the "Pac-o-gram" was so lifelike that audiences seemed to be both amazed and scared in equal measure. The overall stage performance of the Pac-o-gram as the resurrection of Tupac "from the grave," appeared to sit uneasily with audiences and commentators. The performance narrative asked audiences to accept the presence on stage "as Tupac," not a holographic tribute to him. While many enjoyed seeing "Tupac" again, there was also an overwhelming sense of discomfort and a resistance to accepting the hologram as a legitimate stage presence. The reluctance of audiences to fully accept the holographic rendition of Tupac is reflected in the following comments:

> *It was really incredible. I hadn't expected that, but I felt like Tupac was onstage... It just felt a little creepy.*
>
> *Michie Mee, cited by Wong (2012)*

> *Why did Snoop look so scared? Because he knows that his homeboy died more than a decade ago, and to have to be on stage with a hologram would probably trip him out hard.*
>
> *Juan Yahoo Answers (2012)*

> *I loved seeing him again. My mother thought so too, but my aunt really didn't like it because she was really weirded out by it. A lot of people around me don't like it either, and they say it's wrong...*
>
> *Westfesttv (2012)*

> *Technology's getting well scary nowadays. Some freaky ****.*
>
> *Louise, Yahoo Answers (2012)*

The reoccurring theme amongst fan comments was that the Tupac hologram was amazing, but also "freaky," "weird," "scary," and "troubling." So while the performance fascinated and amazed fans, because of its likeness, audiences did not easily accept the hologram as having the ability to "bring a dead artist back to life." Pandalakis expresses this strange interaction between vitality and corporeality. She describes "the hologram as a figure of ambiguity, because of its non-materiality: its transparency points at its virtuality, thus suggesting the absence of a body" (Pandelakis, 2014, p. 6). This suggests that, in this case, the holographic presence teetered dangerously on the precipice of the uncanny valley and, for some, it fell right into the "eerie" category. One fan, who uses the user name Louise, offered a succinct description of this ontological dilemma: "holograms are meant to be all transparent and pixelated and that, and he was even sweating and breathing a lot at the end …" (Louise, 2012, cited in Yahoo Answers, 2012). The presentation of a body that is widely known to be "dead" with signs of life such as breathing and sweating was too much for Louise. Her use of the pronoun "he" as opposed to "it" also indicated that she could not find a comfortable ontological category for the presence—as it looked too alive, yet its referent was too dead.

Much of the conversation surrounding ontological themes in discourses responding to the Tupac hologram lies within the image's attempt to present a "copy" of Tupac's body as it was when the rapper was alive. Baudrillard offers an ominous reading of attempts to "copy" a single human being. With reference to cloning, he suggests that the "double:"

> *... is an imaginary figure, which, just like the soul, the shadow, the mirror image, haunts the subject like his other, which masked it so that the subject is simultaneously itself and never resembles itself again, which haunts the subject like a subtle and always averted death. This is not always the case, however: when the double materializes, when it becomes visible, it signifies imminent death.*
>
> *Baudrillard (1994, p. 95)*

The life-like copy of Tupac in a holographic form not only reminded audiences of what Tupac Shakur was like in life, but the fact that it was a copy of a dead man's body meant the stage presence was also an absence: a representation of a dead referent. This means that the Pac-o-gram is also a reminder of death and human mortality. When the hologram represents a "dead" person's body—and presents it as if it is "alive"—the performer becomes an embodiment of "death" as well as of "life." This death-narrative adds another dimension to the uncanny valley theory, in that the Pac-o-gram was not only too life-like to develop a full affinity for; it was also too ghost-like, and thus invoked its human audience's fears of death as well as the fear of technology becoming too much like human life.

10.4.2 Hatsune

In the case of Hatsune, audience affinity with the vocaloid holographic presence appears to be extremely strong. Her digital DNA, plus an open character narrative, position this holographic performer in the ideal landscape for human attachment. Where popular and academic discourses surrounding the Tupac hologram focus on the "creepy" elements of the holographic copy, the popular commentary on the Hatsune Miku hologram has a positive and celebratory tone. Instead of headlines referring to "legitimacy" and "ethics," as in the case of the Pac-o-gram, Hatsune Miku is considered to be much more than a holographic representation of someone else; she is treated as a performer and a legitimate J-Pop star: a widely recognized "teen pop idol" (Leon, 2012). Compared to the death discourses that are evoked through responses to the Pac-o-gram, popular commentary about the ongoing career of vocaloid Hatsune Miku, focus mainly on a celebration of her "liveness." Thus, themes in audience responses to Hatsune Miku have a very different ontological tone, and suggest that this type of hologram has a secure future on the live music stage.

The paradox in commentary regarding the performances of Hatsune Miku is not in the tension between excitement and fear, as in the case of the Pac-o-gram; rather, fans appear to be torn between a desire for the anime pop star to be a real person and the feeling that she is better than reality, precisely because she is not human, and therefore does not suffer from perceived human failings and imperfections. Journalist Leon quotes one American fan, who sums up the conflicting wish for the hologram to come to life, while not wanting to taint it with "humanness:"

> *I like her a lot more than the other musicians nowadays, because she's not a part of the latest gossip or addicted to drugs or having her 54th baby... But I'm sure that if she was a real person, she would. So I guess I like her more just because she's not real.*
>
> *Ritsu, cited by Leon (2012)*

Fan comments posted on YouTube video World is mine-live HD - Hatsune Miku (Let's Cos Play Till the World Ends, 2014) echo these narratives. Some lament at her artificiality:

> *I know a lot of people say this, and this concert is really good, BUT MIKU WHY AREN'T YOU REAL!*
>
> *(ZerkaBrex)*

> *I feel sad because this is the real world and hatsune miku isn't real and she can't be like a human being.*
>
> *(chris s)*

Others find her to be an improvement, a being that is "better" than human, but no less real:

> *I guess not being a real person is part of all the vocaliod's charm*
> *a charm that says they are better than most real singers.*
>
> *(Natã Valério)*

> *The fact of her no being real also means that she can't die or get addicted to drugs so in my opinion that's way better than having a real singer.*
>
> *(Jadelin McVey)*

> *I was thinking the same way about the drugs, so either way, real or not, SHE IS THE BEST!: D*

Another ontological narrative that overwhelms the conversation is the sophisticated argument for Hatsune's real-ness. Fans legitimate this presence on stage; for them, she is real.

In a strange paradox, the entirely simulated character of Hatsune is "more real" to her fans, than the holographic representation of a rapper who actually lived is to his. This is largely due to the extent to which Hatsune Miku fans are able to participate in the writing of the hologram's "personality." While the company who created the Hatsune hologram have marked her "body" with human-like characteristics, as well as providing the three-dimensional humanoid with a recognizable (yet clearly animated) "appearance," they have not confirmed any one back story for the performer (outside of her live concerts and the technical details of her vocaloid origins). Leon suggests that the lack of context for Hatsune Miku as being anything other than a "performer" means that her "devotees are allowed to see in her whatever qualities they like" (Leon, 2012). The open narrative for Hatsune allows fans to shape their own reality and narrative for her, and their willingness to accept her presence as a legitimate artist is, in part, fuelled by the desires to make their fantasies and stories about her as real as possible too.

The ontological argument attesting to Hatsune Miku's realness is sophisticated and a common thread in online fan discussions. For example, on the ZDNET site, Stewart-Smith (2012) quotes a fan:

...For me she isn't just a bunch of light or synthesizer, but she rather brings joy to many people's hearts like a real person do.

On the YouTube video, Hatsune Miku Live Party 2013 in Kansai, (Raito, 2013) of her concert:

The fact there are people who love her and call her name is proof enough of being alive.

(Kayachlata)

By definition of real, anything could be real if you believe it is, this video is not real it's only instructions being read by a machine but you see it and believe it is real. So yes miku can be real if you believe her to be.

(Dalebaxter)

This animation was made by a human being ... i dont see where the problem is? What do you think how the future will look like? Be amazed by how far our technology has come in this short amount of time.

(Shingeki no Kyojin)

Real or fiction doesn't matter, everything exists... just enjoy what you like:)

(Macblink Skylight)

The difference between Hatsune Miku and, let's say, Lorde, is that while there is zero chance of meeting Hatsune Miku in a coffee shop, the chances of meeting Lorde in one aren't all that much better.

(FALCO64125)

Same thing can be said about god...

(Isaac Pinzon)

Hatsune Miku, as a "not-quite and therefore better" human, positions her clearly in the phase prior to the uncanny valley, where a simulation is just life-like enough for humans to form a deep affinity with it. However, there is also evidence in the Hatsune fan feeds that if the hologram becomes too life-like, the uncanny valley theory will still hold. One fan reflected that:

... with advancements in quantum computing, artificial intelligence and robotics it's inevitable that one day she'll/it'll become "real" or "alive" depending on your definition of real and alive. You could probably have "your own" Hatsune Miku, even though that'll be creepy.

(Marius Rye)
Let's Coz Play till te[sic] world ends (2014)

Therefore, it appears that Hatsune's accepted and celebrated "reality" and thus "liveness" still has its limits, and that these limits could be crossed if the J-Pop star becomes too "alive."

Unlike the Pac-o-gram, Hatsune Miku is not a copy of a person, therefore she is not a "clone" in Baudrillard's spooky spectral sense. As she is not human, she does not raise questions of human mortality and therefore it appears that, as long as she does not become "human," there is little to be frightened of. It seems that her artificiality and fantasy origins lend this particular 3D holographic performer an evolutionary ontology and the vocaloid's "reality" grows at the same rate as her fan-base. Rather than being in the uncanny valley, Hatsune is atop the peak of Mashimoto's affinity model; the balance between her human-likeness, her artificiality and her open "personality." This means that fans use their imagination to write her into their own story and therefore they create their own rules through which to justify her right to be "real." The paradox in popular discourses that argue for the animated simulation's realness and "liveness" when compared to the corresponding focus on death in discussions about the "realistic" hologram of Tupac Shakur is also reflected in the ethical implications of the hologram's presence on the live music stage.

10.5 Ethics

Ethical concerns of ownership and control surround the holographic artist; however, most of these are linked to holograms that refer to a dead artist and present them as if they have come back to life. The ownership of Hatsune Miku's performances is clear, yet interactive. Her vocaloid DNA is owned by the software company, Crypton, and her image was originally created as an avatar to promote the vocaloid product. Fans are fully aware of her origins and her owners and, through this transparency, it appears that fans have little ethical concerns regarding the presentation of her holographic image on stage.

Considering the Pac-o-gram, however, it seems that ethical issues in terms of ownership of the hologram arise as the original owner of the persona, Tupac, has no control over how this image is being used. Drecolias (2014) notes that as the music industry progresses along this path, legal issues surrounding the performance rights of the deceased artist and concerns relating to "intellectual property" may arise, because it is unclear who would benefit if the Tupac hologram went "on tour" (par. 11). Tupac did not choose to perform at Coachella, nor did he select the songs to play, have input in his costume, learn the choreography, or compose the "spontaneous" banter that the hologram addressed the crowd with. Instead of being connected to Tupac, the Pac-o-gram's performance was constructed by Snoop Dog and Dr. Dre. It also appeared in the context of Snoop Dog and Dr. Dre's concert, rather than headlining a show dedicated to Tupac's music. A sense of exploitation of Tupac's image is further reflected in the hugely popular YouTube video of the Pac-o-gram, which is layered with advertisements for Snoop Dog's own website. Thus it appears that Snoop's brand has assumed the control of the reproduction of the Pac-o-gram, garnering extra exposure and advertising space from people interested in seeing the Tupac hologram online. In the comments on the YouTube video, fans cite lyrics from Tupac's *Only God Can Judge Me*, which refer to his beliefs on death. They state:

> *I rather die like a man than live like a coward… R.I.P The Don.*
>
> *(jaws shark, 2014)*

And again:

> *If you guys think Pac is alive then just listen to this quote he says in one of his own songs: "I'd rather die like a man, than live like a coward."*
>
> *(AlwaysRetr0, 2014)*

Fan comments indicate the sense that the Pac-o-gram itself is in opposition to Tupac's remembered persona, especially regarding what his fans believe he stood for in life. Filling an artist's resurrected "image" with the soul of others is ethically questionable, as Montgomery remarks: "the idea of putting recorded dialog in, essentially, Tupac's dead body, for lack of a better term, is kind of troubling because who knows where we go from here?" (National Public Radio, 2012). Fans appear concerned about the detachment of representation from referent, as Tupac himself cannot approve the hologram, and thus there was a considerable conversation about whether the use of his image without his consent was ethically sound.

The fans also found the Pac-o-gram ethically problematic, positioning it as a form of "grave robbing," rather than a resurrection. Their comments illustrate the problem surrounding resurrection of the image of an artist that has been "frozen in time" (Wong, 2012).

> *Part of me wonders what kind of rapper Tupac would have eventually evolved into, for example Snoop is big on rastafarian and Jay-Z has his Frank Sanataria style, can't help but wonder if pac had lived how he would have evolved.*
>
> *(Dannytheman1313, 2014)*

> *I love Tupac but be honest if he came back it would be a big deal but rap in no way is the same anymore it would be different he would have to change his style no more bandannas or cool old skool music…*
>
> *(Omar Perez, 2014)*

> *I'm always thinking if was still alive he would he be different from what he was back then or would he be the same.*
>
> *(AverageOk, 2014)*
>
> *Westfesttv (2012)*

After death, an artist's persona ceases to evolve. Their image is locked and their evolution stops. It is not known how Tupac would have evolved as a rap artist, nor it is known if Tupac would have chosen to perform at Coachella with Snoop Dog and

Dr. Dre at all, and this sits uneasily with the audience. The deceased artist's inability to control representations of their persona after death raises ethical concerns over the creation of a hologram post mortem. Conversations about the Pac-o-gram, and who is profiting from the performance, "overshadows the original artistry" (Wong, 2012) of the rapper to whom the hologram refers.

Fan comments also questioned the integrity of the holographic performance in relation to the original "performer's artistic vision" as it manifested in the "life" of Tupac Shakur. One fan expresses this sentiment in detail:

> *... because [in life] you know he refused to be controlled by the industry, to me they finally found a way to control him. Not to mention am I the only one that feels like it's almost dehumanizing? Like now we don't even have to mourn our dead because they can just be brought back thru hologram. I'd rather watch him on a tv screen behind them than in a hologram. I know I may sound crazy for putting it this way but to me it almost feels like someone's puppet master with the corpse of a legend. Pretty soon they'll have these holograms doing and saying things that the actual person would have never said or done in life. I don't like it...*
>
> *(divalish1, 2013)*
> *Westfesttv (2012)*

The multiple disconnects between perceptions of who Tupac was and what he stood for in life, and the way he was represented in a holographic form, meant that the response to the Pac-o-gram was marked with ethical concerns. In addition to ontological "creepiness" elicited through the hologram's life-like appearance, another deep sense of unease was focused on the notion that external forces were "mastering" a corpse. Overshadowing debates about the ethics of ownership and recreating the image of a dead man was the concern with who controlled the soul, persona, and artistic integrity of Tupac.

Hatsune Miku has an "open" personality, and as such her audience are active participants and co-creators of her "soul." Thus, her fans do not appear to find her holographic form ethically controversial in any way. The audience complicity in the creation of her presence, as well as the transparency of the company who stands to profit from her shows, adds to their overwhelming acceptance of her liveness. As one fan describes:

> *You know the best thing about Miku? Anyone with the software and talent can create a Miku (or other Vocaloid) song.*
>
> *(lehnerus2000, 2012)*
> *Stewart-Smith (2012)*

Unlike Tupac Shakur, Hatsune has no living referent of the "soul," "attitude," or "personality," so it is possible to present her in any way the concert promoters or fans wish without raising any ethical issues. Ironically, it is her non-human aspects—her digitally manipulable image and artificiality—that resonate with her fans and render her a more acceptable presence upon the live music stage.

10.6 Conclusion

While holographic technology offers an exciting future (and present) for the live music stage, it appears that not all holographic artists receive the same level of acceptance. Snoop Dog and Dr. Dre's use of a 3D hologram to resurrect the rapper, Tupac Shakur, for their 2012 Coachella performance was not universally celebrated in the resultant popular media commentary. Analysis of fan comments and news media found that the Pac-o-gram shimmers with dissonance between artist, hologram, and genre. In a genre that prides itself on authenticity and "keepin' it real," the assumption that a technologically altered simulation, claiming to be a well-respected and well-loved dead rapper, would be universally celebrated by Tupac fans was unsubstantiated. Instead the hologram catalyzed a series of conversations regarding the ethics of controlling someone's image after death, without their direct permission.

Ironically, however, the Tupac hologram was criticized for its lack of attention to detail and its inauthentic presentation of Tupac as he would appear had he lived until 2012, but it also frightened some because the image appeared to be "too real" for comfort. The attempt to create "presence" of a dead person seemed only to emphasise Tupac's "absence" on the Coachella stage. From an ontological perspective, Pac-o-gram fell into the uncanny valley for many fans. They were uncomfortable in his life-like appearance, when they knew that Tupac was dead. He was too real to be entirely fake, yet not real enough, because the hologram was not Tupac. The ghostly presence brought to light questions of mortality and simultaneous feelings of awe and unease.

On the other side of the spectrum, an anime hologram, with no single human body as its referent, appears to be fully embraced by her fans and genre. Emerging within a genre that is comfortable with artificiality, Hatsune Miku remains authentic to her image and does not attempt to hide her digital DNA. The live performances of vocaloid superstar Hatsune Miku represent a bridge across the uncanny valley and an avenue through which her human audiences are willing to embrace a technologically born star as real. Hatsune is ethically and ontologically accepted. Her fans feel deeply connected to her "better-than-human" presence and they are willing to advocate for the vocaloid hologram's right to be considered "real." The vocaloid hologram works in tandem with digital and social media technologies, in that the personas of Hatsune, and many others, play on the interactive potential in Web 2.0 software, and allow fans to write themselves into her story. Thus, the vocaloid hologram is a pastiche of fan desires and imaginations: a performer whose personality is open to being whatever her spectator wishes her to be.

So, it appears that the use of technology to create a holographic popstar is an accepted practice within particular generic conventions—as long as the hologram does not appear too human, and thus tainted by the faults that being human brings. However, while resurrecting dead artists is likely to continue to be a part of live performances, the future of this form is complicated with the legalities of copyrighting and owning not just image, but the perceived soul, of an artist—as well as the resultant questions of mortality and death that such a performance raises. Thus it seems that while the hologram is *already* an acceptable presence on the live music stage, genre conventions, performance narratives, and ontological conditions impact on spectator willingness to accept the presence itself as "live."

References

Armstrong, E. (2004). Eminem's construction of authenticity. *Popular Music and Society*, 27, 335–355.

Baudrillard, J. (1994). *Simulacra and simulation*. (S.F. Glaser, Trans.). Michigan: The University of Michigan Press.

Bennett, L. (2012). Patterns of listening through social media: Online fan engagement with the live music experience. *Social Semiotics*, 22(5), 545–557.

Conner, T. (2013). *Masters dissertation: Rei Toei lives!: Hatsune Miku and the design of the virtual pop star*. Chicago, IL: University of Illinois at Chicago.

Crypton Future Media (2014). *Cypton.Net*. Retrieved from http://www.crypton.net.

Drecolias, M. S. (2014). *Tupac and beyond: The implications of the Tupac hologram on copyright and the right of publicity and what it may mean for the future of music*. Retrieved from http://scholarship.shu.edu/student_scholarship.

Forman, M. (2000). Represent: Race space and place in rap music. *Popular Music*, 19(1), 65–90.

Fraley, T. (2009). I got a natural skill…: Hip-hop, authenticity, and whiteness. *Howard Journal of Communications*, 20, 7–54.

Goffman, E. (1959). *The presentation of self in everyday life*. London: Anchor Books.

Goffman, E. (1963). *Behaviour in public places*. New York: The Free Press.

Hosokawa, S. (1999). "Salsa no tiene frontera": Orqesta de la Luz and the globalization of popular music. *Cultural Studies*, 13(3), 509–534.

JiJi, A. F. P. (2014). *Virtual star Hatsune to tour with Lady Gaga*. Japan Times. Retrieved from http://www.japantimes.co.jp/news/2014/04/17/national/virtual-star-hatsune-to-tour-with-lady-gaga-2/#.U9sb:41CXck.

Jones, M. D. (2006). An interview with Michael Eric Dyson. *Callaloo*, 29, 786–804.

Juan. (2012). What'd you think about the Tupac hologram at Coachella? Yahoo Answers (April 16, 2012). Retrieved from https://ar.answers.yahoo.com/question/index?qid=20120416092322AAXBHW0.

Kaufman, G. (2012). *Exclusive: Tupac Coachella hologram source explains how rapper resurrected*. MTV. Retrieved from http://www.mtv.com/news/1683173/tupac-hologram-coachella.

Leon, M. (2012). *Tupac Who?: Hatsune Miku, Japan's hologram pop idol*. The Daily Beast. Retrieved from http://www.thedailybeast.com/articles/2012/04/18/hatsune-miku-japan-s-hologram-pop-idol.html.

Let's Coz Play till te World Ends (2014). *World is mine—live HD—Hatsune Miku*. YouTube. Retrieved from https://www.youtube.com/watch?v=YSyWtESoeOc.

Louise. (2012). What'd you think about the Tupac hologram at Coachella (April 16, 2012). Yahoo Answers. Retrieved from https://ar.answers.yahoo.com/question/index?qid=20120416092322AAXBHW0.

Moody, A. (2006). English in Japanese popular culture and J-Pop music. *World Englishes*, 25(2), 209–222.

Mori, M. (1970). The Uncanny Valley. *Energy*, 7(4), 33–35 (K. F. MacDorman & N. Kageki, Trans 2012). Retrieved from http://spectrum.ieee.org/automaton/robotics/humanoids/the-uncanny-valley.

Nickell, J. (2005). *Secrets of the sideshows*. Kentucky: University Press of Kentucky.

Pandelakis, P. (2014). In the absence of flesh, bodies made anew: Transparancy, avatars and the holographic body in Hollywood cinema (1980–2010). In *Paper presented at the 9th global conference of visions of humanity in cyberculture, cyberspace and science fiction*. Oxford: Mansfield College. Retrieved from http://www.inter-disciplinary.net/critical-issues/wp-content/uploads/2014/05/pandelakisvisionspaper.pdf.

Public Radio, N. (2012). How that Tupac hologram at Coachella worked. *All things considered.* Retrieved from http://0-search.proquest.com.prospero.murdoch.edu.au/docview/1510289101?accountid=12629.

Raito, K. (2013). Hatsune Miku live party 2013 in Kansai. YouTube (May 8, 2013). Retrieved from https://www.youtube.com/watch?v=rL5YKZ9ecpg.

Rolling Stone (2014). *Tupac Shakur Biography*. Rolling Stone. Retrieved from http://www.rollingstone.com/music/artists/tupac-shakur/biography.

Sconce, J. (2000). *Haunted media: Electronic presence from telephony to television*. Durham & London: Duke University Press.

Spencer-Hall, A. (2012). Post-mortem projections: Medieval mystical resurrection and the return of Tupac Shakur. *Opticon1826* (13), 56–71. http://dx.doi.org/10.5334/opt.af.

Stewart-Smith, H. (2012). *Virtual idol Hatsune Miku topping 2012 Olympics poll.* ZDNet. Retrieved from http://www.zdnet.com/blog/asia/virtual-idol-hatsune-miku-topping-2012-olympics-poll/765.

Westfesttv, M. (2012). *Tupac Hologram Snoop Dogg and Dr. Dre Perform Coachella Live.* Retrieved from https://www.youtube.com/watch?v=TGbrFmPBV0Y.

Wong, T. (2012). *Tupac hologram opens up Pandora's box.* The Star. Retrieved from http://www.thestar.com/entertainment/2012/04/20/tupac_hologram_opens_up_pandoras_box.html.

Zhao, S. (2003). *Being there: Concepts, effects and measurement of user presence in synthetic environments*. Amsterdam, the Netherlands: Los Press.

Coda

The motivation for this book began in the corridors of a centre for university teaching and learning at an Australian University, with a request to deliver a guest lecture to Media and Cultural Studies undergraduates on the theme: live music in digital culture. In collaboration, as close colleagues, friends, and fellow cultural studies disciplinarians who were working outside of our original discipline, we found ourselves deeply engaged, and often distracted, by the possibilities that this theme stimulated. We had both researched into music and technology in the recent past, and this simple lecture reignited our shared passion for writing about music, philosophy, and technology.

What started as a casual discussion quickly snowballed into an obsession, and we decided that we needed to produce a book. We extended a call for chapters to friends and scholars, some who we knew personally and others who we thought would have something interesting to contribute to the discussion. We looked especially for people who, like us, felt a deep affinity for music and digital technologies—a mixture of musicians, producers, gamers, and appreciators. We did not stipulate that the authors had to be working in an academic or related professional field. Through the process of editing, it has been our great pleasure to read the diverse perspectives, tones, and genres that extended from a single theme. And we hope that our readers feel the same.

These pieces ruminate not only on what live music means in a digital era but also on how this intersects with unique musical experiences and interests. What we found throughout these musical conversations is that live music—whether experienced face-to-face or online, in the audience or from the stage—has a strong future. Digital culture does not pose a threat to the unrepeatable one-off live music event, rather it acts to augment, promote, and enhance live music experiences, so that the traditional form retains its central position in the gamut of musical experience.

We would like to thank the authors who have helped write and refine the timbre of this book. These musicians, producers, writers, and fans dedicated time and space, mostly outside of full-time working hours, to share their stories, philosophies, and words, which filled the pages of this manuscript with acoustic diversity. Our desire was to create a text that afforded the authors and our readers the opportunity to re-inscribe and reaffirm the meaning and significance of the pleasures gained through the experience of the live music, in any form. We hope this book invites its readers to take the time to better understand themselves in relation to their acts of musical consumption and experience, in the context of the marked, the music, the politics, and the poetic.

Index

Note: Page numbers followed by *b* indicate boxes.

Made in United States
North Haven, CT
03 November 2026

21725934R00089